Investor Relations Handbook

edited by Arthur R. Roalman

Here—in the first book of its type—14 recognized experts take you far beyond the conventional, oversimplified view of investor relations.

Investor relations is not merely building an image, "avoiding the negatives," pestering analysts, or flooding the press with rah-rah news releases. What is it then? This unique book treats investor relations as a precise but complicated science— as well as a rare art full of nuances.

Each chapter has been written by a specialist with impressive credentials and each concentrates on one important aspect of investor relations. Together, their papers add up to the most comprehensive look at the field now available.

The book is full of practical help for the person actively involved in carrying out an investor relations program. For example you will read about . . .

- ☐ the five basic ingredients of a well-rounded investor relations program.
- ☐ how to budget time and expense.
- ☐ the consent method as an alternative to the old-fashioned procedures of an annual meeting.
- ☐ disclosure—the toughest job of the corporate communicator. What facts are material? How and when should they be disclosed?
- ☐ how to handle meetings with analysts.
- ☐ how to "layer" the information in your annual report—for maximum clarity.
- ☐ how to speak the language of the European investor who probably never heard of you (no matter how well known you are on Wall Street).
- ☐ nine very practical suggestions for preparing and placing news material.

And if you want proof that sound investor relations is good for stock performance—you will find it in two detailed case studies of Kaufman and Broad, Inc. and Winnebago Industries. investor relations, the guide includes a list of all essential references.

The current gyrations of the stock market make this book particularly topical. But its wealth of basic philosophy, case studies, and prime references make it a classic.

Investor Relations Handbook

Prepared Under the Auspices
of the
NATIONAL INVESTOR RELATIONS INSTITUTE

Arthur R. Roalman, *editor*

amacom
A Division of
AMERICAN MANAGEMENT ASSOCIATIONS

International standard book number: 0-8144-5349-X
Library of Congress catalog card number: 73-85192

First printing

Foreword

THIS BOOK is based on the premise that an individual is not likely to invest his money—whether it's a thousand dollars, ten thousand dollars, a hundred thousand dollars, or a million dollars—in a corporation's stocks, bonds, commercial paper, or other financial pledges unless he believes strongly that he understands fully what is likely to happen to that corporation in the future. This book also reflects the belief that most investors' willingness to invest in a corporation is influenced by their trust in its management.

Trust isn't built overnight. It is the result of long-term actions by the corporation to provide factual financial information in proper perspective. It is the result of well-grounded, honorable investor relations activities.

Unfortunately, "investor relations" is ill-defined and poorly understood by many managers. Just what is it?

Investor relations is, in fact, a science. There are many laws that specify what must be done and what must not be done. It is also an art. Many unstructured situations with investor relations implications develop in the course of a corporate year. Only extensive experience, a strong commitment to the most honorable relationships with investors, and a management style predicated on the belief that a corporate entity must act in its long-term interests (rather than short-term ones) can develop the best program.

But what—in practice—is investor relations? What is proper and what is improper? What is legal and what is illegal? What is productive and what is wasteful? What investor relations efforts should a corporation undertake? What ones should it avoid?

This book attempts to answer these questions.

What follows is the product of an organization, the National Investor Relations Institute (NIRI), that is dedicated to the concept that corporations must understand and observe both the legalities and the spirit of sound investor relations if they are to be accepted properly in public money markets. The organization is composed mainly of corporate officials who are responsible for investor relations.

All the contributors are members of NIRI, and the book was developed with these audiences in mind:

- [ ] The growing body of professionals directing investor relations for their corporations.
- [ ] The many counselors, attorneys, and investment bankers who provide advice or service.
- [ ] Concerned federal and state officials.
- [ ] Advertising and public relations agencies and employees whose work overlaps into the field.
- [ ] Freelance writers who specialize in business writing.
- [ ] Financial editors of newspapers and magazines.
- [ ] Officials of small- and medium-size companies who conduct some kind of investor relations program.
- [ ] Owners of small businesses who are thinking of going public.
- [ ] Officials of the stock exchanges in the United States and other countries.
- [ ] Educators and students of business and finance.

The audience is wide, but the experience of those who have produced this book is wide enough to meet the needs.

ARTHUR R. ROALMAN

Contents

Part II   Case Histories

Appendix

PART I

Investor Relations

What Is
Investor Relations?

William Chatlos

INVESTOR RELATIONS has grown out of the corporate realization that companies can no longer afford to sit back and assume that performance generates satisfaction among shareholders—existing and potential—and on Wall Street.

A company can produce an extremely successful commodity that satisfies customers and generates earnings; it can have the most harmonious labor relations; it can emulate in marketing and performance what others strive to achieve; but if it fails to communicate to both shareholders and analysts the reasons behind this success and, even more important, that this success will continue, then management is derelict and will inevitably suffer for it.

Investor relations is one of the fastest growing, most precise areas in the world of communications. It is a sophisticated means of reaching and hearing from a diverse audience, and it does *not* entail building up an image or touting a stock.

William Chatlos is Principal, Georgeson & Co., New York, N.Y.

GEARED TOWARD THREE AUDIENCES

Essentially, investor relations is geared toward three audiences—shareholders, potential shareholders, and analysts. Though there are no exact figures available, many companies, including the large blue chip corporations, have been increasing the size of investor relations staffs and enlarging the emphasis placed by senior management on communicating with both investors and Wall Street.

Communicating to investors who already own shares in a company is done through a variety of methods, the annual report and the annual meeting being the primary means employed. However, the concept behind these methods and the methods themselves have lately come under great scrutiny and, as will be discussed, are under enormous pressure to change.

Potential investors are reached by communicating with analysts in brokerage firms or, if the investor is institutional, with analysts employed by the institution.

It has been estimated that 80 percent of the transactions on the major stock exchanges are made on brokers' recommendations that originate with brokerage firms' security analysts. While the status of a company's securities will not be solely dependent on the reactions of security analysts, analysts are an extremely important source of information for investors that cannot be ignored. Companies become particularly aware of analysts' potential power over the securities market when they watch in horror as their stock price plummets after a negative research report is released.

A conservative investor relations program does not necessarily prevent negative research studies, but it can deter them. By communicating frequently with analysts and keeping an open and clean house, management hopefully can avoid surprising the Street with an abnormal increase or drop in earnings. Credibility is the core of a strong investor relations program.

It is important that companies understand that it takes more than publicity to satisfy the needs of the financial community. Shareholders might very well enjoy reading how successful their company is, but as a means of communicating with the company they will still find this unsatisfactory from their particular and perhaps narrow point of view. Shareholders are interested in seeing market results that are compatible with their investment philosophy, and if a shareholder feels that the company is veering away from these goals, he will want to know why.

Suppose a company has been expanding and paying for new plants out of retained earnings rather than by raising new funds through borrowing or new capital issues. To do so, it has had to keep its dividend payout at a relatively low level. Now a new opportunity—perhaps an acquisition—presents itself. Should the company pursue its former course for capitalization and reduce dividend payments even further, or should it, in this instance, seek the necessary funds from outside the business?

Before making the decision, the company must consider the shareholder body. Have most of the shareholders invested in the company because of the dividend it generates, even though at a low level? Or are they concerned with growth of future earnings and would therefore want the expansion funded through retained earnings rather than increased long-term debt?

And what of the investment community? What is its interest in the company? Does it recommend the company for growth or for income?

Essential questions like these must be considered before making important corporate decisions. And if management has failed to communicate in the past with these groups, then the decisions will be even tougher.

Shareholders cannot be taken for granted. Be they your Aunt Jane from Chicago or a large mutual fund, each must be treated correctly and with respect.

Unfortunately, managements often do take their stockholders for granted and view them as a placid body of individuals and institutions who almost always agree with the board of directors and who will rarely rock the boat. Many corporations have taken just this attitude only to find themselves deserted by shareholders who have become disenchanted with the company or who have accepted what seems to be an exceptionally high price for their shares in a takeover attempt. Only then does management ask what it did wrong and look for guidance in relating to its shareholders.

Relating to Wall Street

The investment community is currently undergoing an enormous structural change. Both Congress and the Securities and Exchange Commission have offered plans for innovation in the securities market, and the New York Stock Exchange, under the auspices of its chairman, has also suggested that major changes can be expected in the future.

The number of brokerage houses has been decreasing rapidly in recent years, and this trend is expected to continue. It follows that the number of security analysts has also been dropping, thereby making it increasingly difficult for companies to be followed closely at the initiative of the analyst.

Among the changes that can be expected in the near future are negotiated commissions for all securities transactions, institutional membership on the major stock exchanges, and eventually one interconnected stock market, as opposed to the approximately half dozen currently in operation.

All these innovations will inevitably make an impact on the investor relations programs, whether active or dormant, of publicly held companies. The brokerage community should be communicated with on a regular basis, and managements cannot expect, merely because their company is a publicly held concern, that the Street will naturally have an interest in it.

Analysts are as diverse a group of individuals within a specific business as you are likely to find. Some come from the industries they follow, and others have worked their way up from the back office of a brokerage house. Still others are lawyers or economists who prefer to analyze securities rather than teach or practice.

Companies are classified in a variety of ways by Wall Street, though the "industrial" classification is far and away the most popular. Some analysts prefer to look at smaller, relatively new concerns, whereas others are interested in the large, multinational conglomerates that have sprouted up lately.

Each company of course has its own niche, but the investment community sometimes finds it difficult to classify them precisely. For example, a company that manufactures railroad cars isn't really a transportation company, but it isn't a metals components concern either. There are not that many companies still manufacturing railroad equipment, so a separate industrial classification doesn't exist. The company must then look in the research departments of the different brokerage houses for analysts who would be interested in its particular line.

However, there is a very fine line between communicating new and significant developments and inundating the analyst with large quantities of useless material. Management has to be aware of this subtle difference, for if it thinks that mailing all of its press releases to analysts will endear the company to them, it is sadly mistaken.

By the same token, management must realize that it takes more than two or three meetings a year with forty or fifty analysts to satisfy the needs of Wall Street. Analysts, like any other professional group, succeed in their profession by doing better than their peers, and they will refrain from asking leading questions at a large meeting lest they show their hand. Rather, they prefer to contact management and meet with the company's executives—though not necessarily the chief executive officer—at small meetings on a fairly regular schedule.

RELATING TO THE SHAREHOLDER

Investor relations has evolved as a separate and viable corporate unit in the last three decades because of these many problems and the necessity of dealing with them. In addition, many companies have come to realize in the last few years that a large number of individual shareholders, which may have been the base on which many of them were built, have begun to desert them. While a solid majority of the shares outstanding of all companies still remains in the hands of Aunt Jane, most of the trading done on the exchange is performed by the large institutions, such as insurance companies and mutual funds, and many shareholders are turning away from the stock market and looking elsewhere for potential investment vehicles.

Corporate management has an obligation, both intangible and tangible, to communicate regularly with its shareholder body. Many companies, particularly those with large institutional holdings, will discuss corporate developments with the large shareholder—such as mutual funds or insurance companies—while ignoring, and thereby taking for granted, the smaller shareholder. This mistake can not only damage the company's credibility with Aunt Jane but can prove fatal if a proxy fight or tender offer develops.

An ongoing investor relations program results in a stronger bond between management and stockholders. It is essential that companies remember that even the smallest shareholder owns a "piece" of the company and that he will remain loyal to that company as long as it shows it cares about him by communicating with him.

As a beginning, managements might find it best to explore their initial reasons for going public, even if it was fifty or a hundred years ago, and question whether their goals have been met.

GOING PUBLIC

Obviously the major reason, but not the sole reason, for going public is to raise capital. You have a product or a service which you feel has strong marketing potential but you lack the necessary capital to further explore and exploit this potential. You approach an investment banker and explain your situation to him. A prospectus is then filed with the Securities and Exchange Commission, detailing who is making the stock offering, why it is necessary, and for what purposes the new capital is needed. Also, a detailed background of management's history is needed, as well as a statement about how many of the shares will be owned by management.

This is of course an oversimplification of a fairly sophisticated process. An underwriting must be arranged with other brokers to share in the offering, and a marketplace on which to list the shares must be chosen. The over-the-counter market is usually selected for companies making an initial offering. However, if the company has established itself already and meets the requirements of the two larger exchanges, then it may be listed on either the New York Stock Exchange or the American Stock Exchange.

After all these procedures have been completed, the offering is made. The initial price is chosen by the underwriter as being a fair amount to ask for each share being offered. If the stock is listed over the counter, four or five firms have decided to "make a market" in the stock. That is, they own a large number of shares in the stock and any broker who is looking to buy some shares approaches one of these firms.

After the offering has been completed, the company has a large amount of money, which is what it wanted, and a body of shareholders, which in most cases it doesn't know quite what to do with.

The company is aware that it has to send out an annual report and quarterly progress reports. There is an annual meeting, at which maybe 2 percent of the shareholders show up and for which maybe 60 percent or more have returned proxies.

In preparing the annual report, many companies do not stop to consider the audience. Rather, they portray themselves in the best light possible, either ignoring or playing down negative trends and emphasizing the positive. They also tend to include a large number of impressive photographs on the assumption that the more attractive the report, the more attractive the company.

Most often the company's management wants to get the report printed and out of the way as quickly as possible. It regards the annual report as a necessary burden that requires too much management time.

Unfortunately, many companies not only take this attitude about their annual reports, but they also tend to look on Wall Street with the same disdain. They meet with analysts infrequently, and they have little knowledge of how to organize these meetings on a regular basis or how to communicate with the analysts. These problems are discussed in later chapters in greater detail. Let it now suffice to say that there is more to meeting with analysts than arranging mass meetings at analyst societies.

WHY INVESTOR RELATIONS?

The question of how to maintain a company's image with its stockholders and among analysts is the core of professional investor relations. The relative importance of this image can be examined on a simple level. Assume, for example, that a company wants to make an acquisition. There are a number of ways it can do this, including an outright cash purchase or an exchange of stock. In this case, let's say that it chooses the latter. In this way it can avoid dipping into reserves, and if a large number of shares are held by the company, then a new offering is not needed and the company is that much stronger.

But what if the price of the stock, in management's

opinion, is abnormally low and the company is forced into making a rather poor deal? Why is the price of the stock so low? Why is the market apathetic about the stock?

The company might begin by asking itself how well has it communicated with the Street. When an analyst calls up, is he shunted off to a lower level? Are positive developments communicated to analysts and shareholders, yet negative ones ignored? How much work is put into the annual report and in developing a communications program with the shareholders? If the price–earnings multiple of the stock, that is, the price of the stock divided by the earnings per share, is low, is the major reason for this that Wall Street has heard too little about the company?

During the sixties, when takeover attempts were in their heyday, many companies learned to their chagrin that they had failed to communicate management's capability to their shareholders. Even if the stock was selling at a relatively high multiple, the shareholders barely had second thoughts about selling out to another firm.

This isn't to say that a strong investor relations program will save a company from takeover bids or keep its stock high. However, it will place the company in a good position if earnings begin to make an upturn swing or if another company makes a tender offer.

Also, a strong investor relations program is not to be confused with stock manipulation, which is an attempt by management or another source to push up the price of the stock in order to make money in the market. Investor relations should be built on a base of credibility. The company is stating to its shareholders that it wants to communicate with them. It wants to hear what Aunt Jane thinks of the company and why she chose it as an investment. Management is asking her how it can make its annual report better or what she would like to hear about the company that she hasn't. An investor relations program is saying to the analyst that here is a company that might be worth his attention and that some of his clients might find it to be just the type of investment they are looking for.

Safeco Corp., a leading West Coast financial services company with major insurance interests, recently revamped its entire investor relations program. Prior to the restructuring, Larry Wells, vice president of Safeco, said that the program could best be described by the statement "If anyone really wants to know about the company, they'll find a way. But let's not go out of our way to help them." The problem with the company's investor relations had been that a solid majority of the stock was held by the founders and a few select individuals. Therefore, the company did not think it necessary to try and set up a viable communications program with the remaining shareholders. Unfortunately, Safeco soon discovered that large blocks of shares were being sold on the open market by some of these shareholders.

A new community of shareholders was developing, many of whom had different investment objectives. Some looked to Safeco for its dividends; others saw in the firm a long-term growth potential that would eventually raise the price of the stock considerably. In addition, an acquisition brought a whole new group of shareholders with yet another investment viewpoint.

At this point, Safeco's management realized it had to restructure the investor relations program. As a first step, the company undertook a long-range investor relations program that included visits with analysts around the country, improved means of communicating with its shareholders, and deeper involvement by employees in the firm as an investment vehicle. As was stated by Wells recently, "No matter how excellent a company may be, its survival and growth depend on investor awareness about the company and its future."

The program, which is now approximately four years old, has produced a variety of results. Among them: (1) the number of shareholders is slowly increasing while their average holding is decreasing; (2) after an initial meeting with management, approximately forty analysts expressed interest in following the company; and (3) the number of analysts visiting the company has increased nearly three-fold.

This is not to say that this will happen to any company initiating an investor relations program. However, as an executive officer of the company said recently, while its own problems might not be unique to all companies, the solution could be used by and help anyone.

It is important to keep in mind that corporate management can no longer assume that shareholders will go along with whatever management suggests. The press has carried stories about shareholders voting against executive stock option plans and other management proposals, and in one case shareholders even voted against a stock split.

The shareholder is no longer passive, silent, or indifferent. As increased holdings of institutions make their impact on the traditional management–shareholder relationship, the whole area of shareholder relations is bound to alter considerably.

Few companies really know their stockholders. This in itself is a paradox of good public relations techniques. A public relations department properly devotes much of its energy to studying and researching its "publics" prior to planning its activities. Yet many companies expect to have good stockholder relations programs without researching or knowing their stockholders at all.

Some investor relations practitioners emphasize communication with the press as an important segment of corporate development. Financial writing is a diverse sector of journalism whose coverage of Wall Street runs the gamut from the rudimentary to the sophisticated, and shareholders and analysts read many publications on a regular basis.

However, companies would be wise not to depend solely on the press in developing a communications program with the investment community.

KNOWLEDGE OF SHAREHOLDER THINKING

A knowledge of shareholder thinking is not quickly or easily acquired. It should be compiled over a period of years, but few companies have the foresight to actively seek such information.

Effective survey techniques can supply management with valuable information that should be used as a basic platform for the stockholder relations program. It is doubtful that an effective program could be formulated to influence and inform shareholders without prior research of their opinions, attitudes, and informational levels on such questions as dividend policy, evaluation of management, financial status, characterization of the stock, readership of company communications, market price of the stock, and the desire to hold or dispose of the stock in the future. Personal data about stockholders should be obtained, including age, education, income, occupation, and years of stock ownership.

There are a variety of ways to gather this information.

In addition to phone and mail surveys, one relatively inexpensive method would be to include a questionnaire in the company's annual report, assuming management is sufficiently sophisticated to avoid making policy decisions based on the marginal reliability of such surveys.

The information obtained could provide the initial step in an investor relations program. The company could proceed to set up analyst meetings, possibly communicating to the analyst the type of shareholder body it has. In addition, it could gear its corporate publications toward its specific audience, rather than prepare them for a mass audience.

There should be little doubt that accurate, unbiased information about stockholders is a fundamental prerequisite to effectively telling a company's story to both stockholders and analysts. By updating this material every few years, the company is also able to judge how successful the investor relations program has been.

A company executive, while recently discussing his investor relations program, said that the company had come to learn two things about dealing with analysts: tell only that which realistically can be delivered, and tell both the good and the bad, both early and straight.

Don't Expect Overnight Miracles

Companies initiating an investor relations program should not expect overnight miracles. After a group of analysts has met with management, the chances are that they are not going to run back to the office and put out a "buy" on the stock. Having reviewed the record, they'll want to watch the company in action and see how it does under economic conditions the analyst can keep an eye on. Once the firm has proved itself to him, the analyst will then do something with the stock.

The analyst shouldn't be pestered but, rather, be kept in touch with new and significant developments. Most important, he should not be given information not previously released that could have a material effect on earnings. Not only is he forbidden to use it by law, but if he has done any work on the stock at all, it is totally down the drain because of his inside information.

The law governing investor relations has grown quite sophisticated in recent years, particularly in the realm of disclosure, and many people expect it to become even more important in the future. So far, analysts, lawyers, accountants, public relations executives, and even a newspaper columnist have been charged with illegally using undisclosed corporate news or with slanting the news. This topic is covered in greater detail in a later chapter entitled "Investor Relations and the Law."

A wide variety of corporate literature is produced by companies for the investment community, but the annual report is the most important yearly document any company will produce, simply because it is the guide that shareholders and analysts alike will use to judge the performance of the company. Quarterly reports also are important, and they should not be prepared in a haphazard fashion.

Rather than issuing the normal interim statements, some companies have initiated sending earnings releases to shareholders and analysts as well as the press so that the investment community can be kept up to date on the company's progress. The interim statement, which contains essentially the same information plus comments from the company's president, is also sent to these same groups approximately one month later.

Investor relations has changed considerably during the last decade. Instead of taking the shareholder body for granted, management is coming to appreciate the influence that stockholders can have over the company, and innovations have been introduced to give them a greater say in the management of the firm.

The annual meeting, the granddaddy of all investor relations, has come under close scrutiny by a number of firms, and one company, Fuqua Industries, Inc., has even called for its abolishment, labeling it an archaic tradition that serves no purpose for either management or the shareholders.

About five years ago, General Electric found that its annual meeting was becoming unwieldy because of the enormous amount of time taken up by the statutory requirements. The company decided to set up two annual meetings, one in the spring, during which the statutory requirements could be met and the stockholders could present their views, and one in the fall, which was to be a shareholders information meeting. At the latter gathering, management would present to the shareholders the current status of the company and would respond to their comments and questions.

The move to a dual-meeting format has been quite successful. The two meetings are scheduled so that they are located in the same city during a one-year period, then switched to another part of the country the following year.

It is innovations like this that have helped to change investor relations from a minor duty of the public relations department to an important part of the overall corporate structure.

The future of investor relations will reflect an upsurge in the number of corporate programs being initiated. Outside counseling firms in investor relations have begun to proliferate, and public relations concerns are coming to realize that relating to the investment community is more than a blizzard of optimistic news releases and stories in the media.

The increasing concern of the government, particularly the SEC, about investor relations will of course have an enormous impact on communications programs geared toward shareholders and Wall Street. Not only will it be necessary for corporate management to keep abreast of the changes the government might instill, but it must also have an idea of where the government might turn next.

There is no mystery about investor relations. There is no magic formula for communicating with shareholders or Wall Street. Investor relations is constructed around the corporate desire to relate and communicate with those individuals who have the most concern about the future of a company.

How to Budget
Dollars and Time

Gerald A. Parsons

IN SETTING OUT to budget the time and expense of carrying out an investor relations program, as in any planning process, the first important step is to establish objectives.

The next step is to determine who in the corporation shall be involved in the program and what the role of each person involved shall be. In some companies, the job of the investor relations officer is to serve as the chief spokesman to the financial community, to spare the rest of the management the burden investor relations might otherwise place on them. In other companies, he may be the individual who arranges contacts between management and interested members of the financial community. Ideally, he is a combination of the two: as an effective company spokesman he removes the burden of day-to-day contact from the shoulders of busy operating and corporate staff executives; at the same time he selectively arranges for direct contact

---

Gerald A. Parsons is Director, Financial Relations, Champion International Corporation, New York, N.Y.

with appropriate management representatives when this can add to the overall effectiveness of the program.

To achieve effectiveness in his roles, the investor relations officer must have the kind of credibility that can result only from being kept thoroughly informed on the operations, plans, and prospects of the company. He must be a true representative of top management, and he must be communicative. If he is not, persevering analysts will seek ways around him to obtain the information they think they need.

There are typically five basic ingredients in a well-rounded investor relations program, and the objectives established for the program will determine the amount of emphasis placed on each. They are:

Individual direct contacts with members of the investment community

Group meetings

Formal presentations (including field trips)

Mailing of printed material

General publicity, including advertising

In budgeting for all of the above, it has become essential in most companies to designate some individual to be the chief spokesman to members of the investment community.

In some cases, this may be the chief executive officer or head of the corporate staff. But in more and more cases, a full-time investor relations officer has assumed this responsibility. In a very large corporation the job may require more than one man. Certain aspects of the job may be incorporated into other company activities, such as advertising or public affairs, but there should be a clear understanding of the functions and responsibilities of each department.

INDIVIDUAL CONTACTS

In budgeting for the type of individual who can effectively represent top management, it should be borne in mind that he must not only be an effective communicator but have several other qualifications as well. He needs a basic understanding of accounting and finance, and he must be capable of winning the respect of bright, well-educated, discerning, and sometimes aggressive security analysts.

In most companies today, this places him fairly high on the organizational ladder, with corporate officer or equivalent status. In smaller companies, or those just starting an investor relations program, he may be a corporate officer with other duties. And there are certain large corporations that have two or more full-time people who serve as direct contacts with financial analysts, with additional people assigned to institutional investor contact, investor meeting planning, investor publications, and so on.

Individual contacts can be limited to visits to the investor relations officer in his own offices, or they can include visits with other company officers or operating representatives. In addition, the well-rounded program will probably include visits by the investor relations officer and possibly other members of management to investors in financial centers throughout the country, and, increasingly, in Europe and Japan.

GROUP MEETINGS

An effective means of getting management exposure to important members of the financial community is the informal group meeting. Such meetings can be initiated and/ or arranged by the company, by a friendly broker or investment banker, or by a group of analysts who specialize in the industry in which the company is engaged. Typically, the latter are called "splinter groups" (having split off from the major security analyst societies to better serve their members' interests) and are limited in membership to twenty or thirty analysts. The best group meetings are generally kept fairly small and informal, with a minimum of prepared presentation and plenty of time for open questions and answers. Perhaps the best meetings of this type are organized independently by the company, provided the appropriate audience is identified and can be invited on an individual basis.

In budgeting for such meetings, it's possible to get off quite inexpensively, especially if they are sponsored by an outsider. They require little more than the time of the executives who participate. If self-sponsored, the major expenses are for the physical arrangements, which can range from a breakfast meeting to a straightforward, no-nonsense presentation during business hours in the conference room at company headquarters, or to a cocktail and dinner affair at a good club or hotel.

FORMAL PRESENTATIONS

Perhaps the most common type of formal investor relations presentation is that which is made before the major security analyst societies throughout the country. The New York Society of Security Analysts is the largest and most prominent. This group meets every business day, and normally the luncheon meetings are attended by a hundred or more interested member analysts. Attendance by fifty to a hundred analysts is not uncommon in some other cities, such as San Francisco, Chicago, or Boston. The New York society and some of the others have enlarged their programs to include afternoon industry forums, dinner meetings, and field trips to company locations. Most major society meetings are now covered by national press representatives, but it's usually possible, at almost any meeting, to arrange for special press coverage by holding a press conference in conjunction with the meeting.

The alternative to security analyst society meetings is, again, the company-planned and -sponsored presentation. This can be held at a convenient hotel or club, at company headquarters, or at an operating location where a tour of plant operations, research facilities, or other points of interest can be included.

In budgeting for formal presentations, it is possible to limit expense to the time it takes to prepare a written talk. Since one of the key advantages of such presentations is the fact that they may attract national press coverage, it is essential that they be prepared in advance and reproduced for distribution at the time of the meeting. It may be advantageous to expand the presentation to include visual aids, and the cost of preparing slides, props, or displays can vary from nominal to many thousands of dollars. One well-known company holds several investor relations meetings a year in which there are formal presentations throughout the better part of a day. One typical fifteen-minute talk may include as many as a hundred professionally produced color slides or a filmstrip.

When a company-sponsored meeting is held at a remote location, it is sometimes appropriate that the company underwrite the cost of transportation to and from the meeting by the participants. However, the benefits the participants derive are usually considered sufficient to attract good attendance at their own expense, and the company is then expected only to provide whatever food, refreshments, or local transportation good taste dictates.

MAILINGS

Most security analysts are literally deluged with reading material, including newspapers and magazines, trade journals, government publications, and mailings from the companies they follow (and many from those they don't). This prompts a rather careful preparation and selection of mailings to attract the most favorable attention and achieve the best comprehension.

Perhaps the most important consideration is timing. If a news release is made in time to appear in the next morning's newspapers, it is often possible to mail the release in time for it to arrive on many analysts' desks the same day it appears in the press. If they missed it in the paper, they'll have it in their mail. If the press fails to give complete coverage of the story, they will have the full text of the release.

Examples of material that is generally of interest would naturally include the quarterly and annual results, news of acquisitions and mergers, announcement of new products or discoveries, change of management, news of economic factors affecting the business, and similar timely information.

Of course, no mailing is possible without a mailing list. As in the selection of the amount of time that will be spent with which individual analysts, the determination of what mailings will be sent to which analysts is a subjective judgment. Theoretically, all "material" investment information will be made available to the general public simultaneously through the recognized news services. In all practicality, it is possible to pick out those analysts who have a special interest in the news of the company on a continuing basis. For most companies, their number is relatively small.

While it would probably be possible to divide the mailing list into a number of categories, according to readers' specialty or investment role, or degree of probable interest, for example, it seems practical to divide the list into at least two, and possibly no more. This would break down into those who are known to be interested in the company in detail and those who only want to be kept generally informed. To the first group you would send all your mailings, and to the second you would send only your annual reports, quarterlies, and other broadly distributed documents. Naturally, this is a matter of choice and will depend most on the communications philosophy of your company.

Budgeting for mailings is pretty straightforward. Multiply the number of mailings planned by the number of people on your mailing list(s) by the average cost per mailing. The latter is where budgeting can easily become less precise. A two- or three-page news release is simple—a routine reproduction job, a No. 10 envelope, and normal postage. On the other hand, if you should decide to mail your 10-K, and it's fifty pages long and multilithed on legal-size paper, that's another story. In this case, it may be advantageous to think in terms of additional printing cost in order to save money on mailing.

The cost of maintenance of the mailing list can also vary considerably, depending on who does it and how many names are on it. There are many commercial mailing services that supply selective lists covering the functional and industry specialties of a variety of classes of recipients.

There is so much mobility among members of the financial community that it is both difficult and important to pick a mailing service that keeps its lists up to date. Experience is likely to lead to the decision to make up and maintain your own list. Even then, it will probably be possible for an enterprising mailing service to come up with important potential recipients whom you've missed.

Regardless of whether you choose a mailing service or the do-it-yourself approach, an annual survey, in addition to normal day-to-day changes as you learn about them, is essential to the effectiveness of the program.

There is one final word about a mailing program that may be of considerable long-term value—the desirability of adding a personal touch to the mailings. Although the piece being mailed may be a straight news release or printed item that will otherwise get broad distribution, a personalized tip-on or covering letter may make the difference between whether the item is read or not. This is also an effective way to call attention to the important points covered in the mailing. Finally, it should give the recipient a point of personal contact if he has any questions. Often such questions prompt a telephone review of operations and outlook, or a valuable personal visit.

GENERAL PUBLICITY

Any publicity the company receives, whether in general news media, magazine articles, product advertising, speeches by company representatives, or what have you, can be assumed to generate either a direct or an indirect investor relations impact. In fact, anything that affects the company image will have some kind of effect on investor attitudes toward the company—sometimes more than is realized.

In some companies, all the functions of public affairs, including investor relations, are combined within one organizational component. Theoretically, this should insure that investor relations considerations are factored into the planning and preparation of all news releases, promotional material, advertising, or other printed communications. This is not always true, however, and when investor relations is a separate function, or when it is part of the financial organization, the possibility of overlooking these important considerations is apt to be greater unless safeguards are established.

The most common problem in this connection is the natural inclination of publicists to put the company's best foot forward and to "avoid the negatives." This can lead to a lack of credibility for materials that are considered to be too PR-oriented.

Perhaps the more serious problem occurs when emphasis is placed on news that might normally be expected to be positive but turns out to be negative so far as investor attitude is concerned. Take as an example a company's announcement of a new plant or entry into a new market. The company may be completely justified in its decision economically, but certain industry specialists who do not have all the facts feel that such new capacity or competition may be dilutive, that it may result in "breaking the market" or lowering general profitability in that particular field.

If this potential negative reaction is anticipated in advance, through consultation with the investor relations officer, it may be possible to present the story in a manner that will be better understood and favorably accepted.

Finally, a good mailing program will include the distribution of certain publicity materials that may be of particular interest to analysts. If there appears to be any danger of misinterpreting, or need for amplification of the message, this can be handled in the investor relations man's tip-on.

Budgeting time and expense for investor relations is really no different from budgeting for any other staff operation. It requires good planning backed by a thorough understanding of objectives. Once the plan is in effect, perhaps the most important key to success is periodic assessment of accomplishments, reassessment of goals and objectives, and adjustment of plans and budgets to meet them.

No investor relations program will work well, or for long, unless management gets solidly behind the program, gives the person responsible the informational back-up required, and maintains scrupulous integrity. When these ingredients are added to good planning, the results will be both rewarding and thoroughly enjoyable.

Where Investor Relations?

Alan M. Singer and Marvin A. Chatinover

BECAUSE directors are elected to represent the interests of shareowners, it would seem proper that the board should formulate the policies that govern relations between the corporation and the investor.

But in actual practice it is the officers of a company, and particularly the chief executive officer, who speak to the public, investment professionals, and the communications media and who are the most visible symbols of the company to shareowners. Consequently, the philosophy and objectives of the chief executive officer are usually a controlling factor in the formulation and execution of investor relations programs and activities.

At one extreme, such a philosophy might be a purely legalistic view that shareholders are entitled to whatever information about company affairs management is required

Alan M. Singer is Principal, Alan M. Singer & Co., Buffalo, N.Y.; Marvin A. Chatinover is Director, Corporate Relations, Moore and McCormack Co., Inc., New York, N.Y.

by regulatory authorities and regulations to make available to them, and that if investors are dissatisfied they can simply sell their shares or band together to change management.

More affirmative philosophies would recognize that strong investor relations programs emphasizing a full and continuous flow of information about the company can help lower the cost of capital in the securities markets and develop and maintain goodwill among shareholders, who will thereby be encouraged to support management. This latter is a factor that can be quite important, for example, in the face of a takeover bid or other external threats. In addition, such efforts can help win greater approval from other publics that the corporation must deal with, including customers, employees, and governments.

Because management is required, apart from its philosophical bent, to conduct some investor relations activities, the chief executive officer and the board of directors must clearly define the basic functions and responsibilities of investor relations that are to be performed. These would include, at minimum, the following activities:

Legal–Secretarial

Official filings

Review of proxy materials and documents relating to such matters as mergers, tender offers, acquisitions, and changes in capitalization

Supervision of transfer agent and registrar

Financial

Preparation of public reports of operations and financial condition

Statements of financial policy and objectives

Communications

Reports to shareholders

News releases of all "material" information

Planning of annual meetings and other public forums on corporate financial matters

Shareholder correspondence

It is therefore evident that the broad span of investor relations activities requires diverse skills and temperaments that must be carefully organized and directed to facilitate fulfillment of the company's investor relations objectives.

Management must determine such targets. Specific objectives, such as the development and maintenance of an appropriate multiple of earnings power reflected in the market price of the company's stock, will require the development of certain strategies and selection of appropriate practices and methods.

For example, an effort directed at improvement of the price–earnings ratio would involve, among other things, formulation of a plan to increase knowledge of the company among securities analysts and other professionals in the investment community. The plan should incorporate a judicious strategy aimed at developing rapport with those professionals who are most likely to have an interest in the company because of their particular fundamental preferences, portfolio requirements, or other significant considerations, such as market liquidity.

If greater geographical distribution of shareholdings were also an objective, plans should be made for contacting professionals in major securities markets throughout the nation. Such an effort might also call for stimulating greater individual investor interest through revisions in corporate literature aimed at enhancing the attractiveness of the company and in financial and corporate publicity efforts aimed at increasing public awareness of the company.

Because investor relations is, in fact, a vital form of communication of the company itself that can produce tangible consequences of considerable magnitude, it should ideally be a separate staff function reporting directly to the chief executive officer.

From a managerial standpoint, a separate department headed by an executive of at least vice presidential rank has definite advantages. It permits the chief executive officer to assess the cost and effectiveness of investor relations activities in the most efficient manner. Moreover, the position of such a staff in the corporate hierarchy tends to attract persons of high caliber who are most likely to develop the kinds of ongoing programs that can generate desirable results for the company.

Although at least half the members of a small group of well-compensated investor relations executives (average annual salary is over $40,000) indicate that half their members report to the president and/or chief executive officer of their respective companies, this is not common practice. Such allocations of responsibility are not widespread even among very large corporations where the frequency and volume of investor relations activities would argue strongly for a separate staff function.

In fact, surveys by the Financial Executives Institute indicate that because of the traditional role of finance in the procurement and management of capital, the investor relations officer in many corporations reports more frequently to the chief financial executive.

The rationale for such a structure can be persuasive. Although investor relations is a communications activity, the sophisticated substance of the activity must receive emphasis beyond the form of communication. Hence it is felt by some that financial management is the logical choice to direct the investor relations function. Such a structure exists, for example, in Champion International, where the director of investor relations reports directly to the financial vice president, who in turn reports to the president. A similar structure exists at Warner-Lambert, where the director of finance has the responsibility for investor relations. On the other hand, General Electric, which has a well-earned reputation for the quality and volume of its investor relations activities, views the function as a component of its total communications efforts to all publics, with the manager of investor relations reporting to the vice president of public affairs.

Actually, the responsibility for various investor relations functions tends to be split. Thus in some companies the secretary will handle shareholder reports in addition to official filings, talk to security analysts, and make recommendations to the chief executive officer on important investor relations policy matters.

Split responsibilities for individual functions of course

make coordination and consistency of investor relations efforts difficult from a managerial viewpoint. In such cases, the effectiveness of investor relations activities may depend more on rapport between various staff functions and personal goodwill between executives than on traditional methods of organization and accountability.

Many companies use outside counsel to conduct their investor relations activities or to supplement those handled internally. Because of third-party status, competent external counsel can be particularly useful in helping to assess credibility problems in the financial community and also to give management independent judgments concerning controversial problems on which internal executives may be reluctant to speak with complete candor.

In some cases, management takes the position that the limited scope of its investor relations activities does not justify a separate department or specialized assignments. To develop and maintain some semblance of efficiency and consistency, joint direction may be under the aegis of a group consisting of executives responsible for individual investor relations functions. Such a team might consist of the chairman of the board, the chief financial executive, the secretary, and the director of public relations.

If a chief executive officer is vitally concerned about fulfillment of investor relations objectives, he may assume personal direction of the task, assigning such duties as writing reports and preparing speeches to selected aides. The latter, of course, may be staff executives, such as the chief financial officer and the director of public affairs. The chief executive officer frequently heads the management team in addressing large groups of security analysts; he may even choose to meet personally with analysts who visit the company. From the standpoint of consistent development of policy, the investor relations executive should counsel the chief executive officer with respect to all such meetings and personally attend each one.

The organization of investor relations activities is usually determined by the volume of related communications being generated by the company. This in turn is related to the number of shareowners and investment professionals with whom contact is maintained and the degree of company interest in developing and improving its investment position. The latter, of course, reflects the philosophy of the chief executive officer.

The ability of a company to develop and execute a meaningful investor relations program depends in no small measure on the procurement of appropriate executive talent.

Examination of the minimum investor relations functions indicates quite clearly that an executive in this area should have an acute perception of the financial and legal aspects of corporate policy and a strong awareness of the interests of certain key publics, such as shareowners and the professional investment community, in those functions of the company. Equally important is an ability to communicate such matters responsibly and clearly in a way that is consistent with the needs of the company and its audiences and that satisfies all appropriate statutory and other disclosure regulations.

But the combination of financial executive, lawyer, and public relations expert is difficult to find in one person. At best, a company has a right to expect some education, such as business school training, thorough knowledge of the legal implications of disclosure regulations and general grounds for stockholder litigation, and an ability to articulate such matters from the viewpoint of the company's investor relations policy.

Budgetary considerations loom large in deciding the structure and placement of investor relations activities within the company. Executives who possess the range of abilities noted above are now receiving from $30,000 to $75,000 yearly. This includes investor relations executives who report to the chief executive *indirectly* through the finance or public information functions.

It must be recognized, however, that because of budgetary reasons, management may place primary reliance on other executives to carry out investor relations activities that are in line with their own staff functions or on external consultants with specialized capabilities.

In any case, a company must be aware of the judgment skills and time requirements for successful execution of investor relations functions. With due respect for budgetary realities, the dilution of investor relations efforts through their appendage to other vital and busy staff functions may, in fact, prove more costly in the long run. This can be seen through closer examination of essential investor relations activities.

In contacts with securities analysts, other company officers may lack the investor relations officer's degree of understanding of the problems surrounding disclosure of material information. This does not suggest that the investor relations officer is more important than legal counsel. But the company should recognize, as have some experts on communications law, that those skilled in the perception of corporate communications may be better judges of what constitutes materiality in a given situation.

Similarly, though the financial executive is clearly the staff expert on financial matters, the investor relations officer is acutely aware of the needs and wants of the security analyst in this area. By counseling and helping to prepare written communications on financial matters, the investor relations officer may be better able to help the company achieve certain vital objectives, such as maintenance of a fair multiple, than an officer who must meet diverse reporting needs for financial data.

In corporate publications ranging from annual reports to news releases, the investor relations officer is more cognizant than his public relations counterpart of the particular nuances of corporate policies that affect shareowners.

This is not to gainsay the importance of communications skill per se. Indeed, in such companies as Champion International and Warner-Lambert, the public relations staff issues financial news releases and works on the annual report. These activities, of course, are reviewed by investor relations to insure that they are consonant with the needs of shareowners and the financial community, as well as with the company's investor relations policy objectives.

But for such communications tasks as the preparation of speeches to securities analysts, for the annual shareholders meeting, or to other groups with particular interest in financial matters, the investor relations officer may be presumed to have superior relevant background.

Although 10-K statements, prospectuses, and other official filings are primarily legal documents, they are increasingly being regarded, especially by the SEC, as communications too. Indeed, the Commission has been urging greater clarity in the presentation of financial data and the use of graphics in prospectuses to enhance their effectiveness as tools in the marketing of securities. Clearly, these documents call for the application of investor relations skills.

Correspondence from shareowners demands appropriate responses on matters of corporate policy that affect investors. This too is a logical responsibility for investor relations experts.

A company should know where its stock is being traded and by whom. Knowledge of such factors as the geographical pattern of stock ownership, the existence of strong friendly holdings that management can rely on in case of external challenges, the availability of and desire for blocks of company stock—all have a direct bearing on the objectives of investor relations policy. These would include plans to vary the distribution of stock, to combat potential tender offers and to spot advantageous opportunities for purchase of stock for use in internal option and/or retirement plans, or to reduce the number of outstanding shares to increase per-share earnings. And these are matters that logically come within the scope of investor relations.

Successful execution of investor relations functions will depend, to a great extent, upon the credibility of the officer and personnel who perform these activities. That credibility will in turn reflect the capabilities and integrity of the investor relations professionals and of corporate policy and objectives.

The investor relations executive, for instance, must possess sufficient acquaintance with related disciplines, including accounting, financial management, law, and communications, to be able to talk about the company authoritatively to security analysts and other sophisticated audiences. And the company must allow him sufficient access to information in these areas to insure that his external communications efforts will be authoritative. It is damaging to the credibility of the company, not just the individual, to have an investor relations executive embarrassed by surprises. One way to avoid such situations is by frequent and direct access to the chief executive officer so that he may be made fully aware of all major policy trends.

A company, in turn, should demand a minimum level of skill consistent with its own investor relations philosophy and objectives. The investor relations executive also should possess the essential ingredients of integrity and suitable temperament for the work. His reputation for integrity will have a direct bearing on the success of his activities vis-à-vis professionals such as securities analysts and the financial communications media. Because of the broad scope of investor relations and the increasing professionalization of the field, a company should encourage and expect its executive to participate in such organizations as the National Investor Relations Institute and to maintain an active pursuit of knowledge in the developing body of literature in investor relations as well as in the closely related areas of finance, accounting, law, and general management.

Moreover, the investor relations executive must be constantly aware of new developments in legal obligations and restrictions pertaining to corporate financial communications.

Proper temperament is essential for successful performance as an investor relations officer. Conservative demeanor, for example, is usually preferable for establishing personal credibility with the financial community. Even if the investor relations executive reports directly to the chief executive officer, his department must draw upon the knowledge and skills of other staff functions, such as finance, the secretary, public relations, and possibly the board, whose members may serve as valuable contacts with key people in the financial community and with certain large stockholders. As in all such intracorporate relationships where direct authority is lacking, the executive who desires the input of others will have to exercise persuasive, diplomatic skills of his own.

However, it should be remembered that the ability of the investor relations executive to gain such assistance will also reflect his personal status in the corporate hierarchy, which in turn will be a function of the general corporate philosophy with respect to investor relations policy and objectives. The greater the significance accorded it by the chief executive officer and the board, the greater will be the opportunity for the investor relations executive to be truly effective.

In brief, the quality of effort and talent that a company should expect in investor relations is directly related to its policy orientation. The greater the realization of the potential long-term economic benefits of a sound program, the more likely a company is to plan and structure an appropriate investor relations function.

The Annual Meeting: Pro and Con

Edward H. Muncaster

"THE CONTINUED PRACTICE of having an annual ritual which we represent to be a meeting of the stockholders is a farce, if it is not, indeed, a fraud." This is the opinion of J. B. Fuqua, chairman and chief executive officer of Fuqua Industries, Inc., Atlanta, writing in the business and finance section of *The New York Times,* Sunday, April 23, 1972.

"My personal view is that the corporate annual meeting is and should continue to be the basic forum of shareholder democracy and an important stimulus to candid corporate self-analysis," said James J. Needham, chairman of the New York Stock Exchange, in a speech to corporate presidents, Chicago, December 7, 1972.

The role of the annual meeting in the field of investor relations is a unique one. It is certainly the oldest vehicle that has been used to inform stockholders, and it is a practice that precedes the relatively new professions of investor

Edward H. Muncaster is Vice President, Gardner, Jones & Company, Inc., Chicago, Ill.

relations, corporate and financial public relations, and even the textbook catchall, corporate communications.

Today the annual meeting is still the most widely practiced investor relations function for the reason that it is required by state articles of incorporation and individual company bylaws. These statutory provisions require a meeting of the owners of an incorporated business to vote on management and stockholder proposals affecting the structure of the business. Such laws apply not only to publicly held firms listing thousands of individual owners but to privately owned firms where ownership of the company can rest with few stockholders.

Such meetings have become an acknowledged corporate tradition that has grown with our economic system. Beginning in colonial times, stockholder meetings have flourished in an unbroken pattern along with the realization of a people's capitalism in which everyone is encouraged to own a share of American industry. While neither the SEC nor the stock exchanges have written requirements calling for an assembly of stockholders, the SEC does ask that the announcement of the annual meeting be disclosed, and the NYSE and other exchanges have had an "implicit understanding" with their member companies that an annual meeting will be held.

The practice of stockholder meetings is, however, a subject that brings forth a dramatically wide range of opinion and response from corporate management. At one end of the spectrum are those who regard the annual meeting as a hallmark of corporate democracy and an expression of our free enterprise system. At the other are those who look upon the function as a meaningless corporate exercise and are taking bold steps to eliminate it altogether. Between the two extremes are varying corporate attitudes of annoyance, indifference, indulgence, resignation, and acceptance.

In Support of the Annual Meeting

Proponents of annual meetings see both tangible and intangible benefits accruing from the considerable efforts such meetings entail. For a management with a desire to communicate, the meeting can serve as a publicity platform for national and international media attention through the release of material information. A positive approach to the affair will insure that the local press and national wire services are encouraged to be present. Special accommodations may be provided media members, in addition to the preparation and distribution of a news release covering the events and informational content of the meeting. Extra time may be allocated for a press conference or individual interviews with company officers.

Besides being of value as a publicity outlet, the annual meeting carries with it the occasion to reach all shareholders via printed material through a postmeeting report. This can be a welcome addition to the standard corporate annual and interim reports. The postmeeting report is of special value to the great majority of stockholders unable to attend the meeting because of geographic limitations, and it has the potential to be an important communications vehicle for all public audiences of the corporation, including financial analysts. In addition to a summary or even a complete transcript of management's presentations, questions and answers occurring between management and the audience can be included. Since most annual meetings are held three to four months after the close of the fiscal year, management interested in preparing an informative presentation may include first-quarter corporate results and perhaps some insight into the company's outlook for the year. If this is done, an annual meeting report might be combined with the first-quarter interim statement to stockholders.

For a company located in a small or medium-size city, or even a distinct neighborhood of a large metropolitan area with a high concentration of stockholders, there can be an additional community relations value in a strong annual meeting effort. At the same time, such locations may attract an above-average number of stockholders who are company employees. In these circumstances, management is apt to make the affair as accessible as possible, perhaps holding the meeting on a weekday evening or on Saturday. By opening the meeting to the general public, attendance can run high, and it is not unusual in smaller communities for entire families to make the activity a day's outing. Where encouraging rather than limiting attendance is the objective, there are as many different approaches as there are companies in question. A letter of invitation from the president or chairman of the board, in addition to the usual notice of meeting, proxy, and proxy statement, is a personal gesture. A luncheon or some kind of reception following the meeting, a tour of nearby facilities, and free transportation can help to promote stockholder interest.

Annual meeting advocates are likely to be found in the consumer products area where the belief exists that stockholders are potential customers and vice versa. Elaborate displays, handouts, and product demonstrations prevail. Certainly a manufacturer of sports equipment or small household appliances has the potential for a more interesting, colorful, and more personally relevant annual meeting from the stockholders' point of view than a manufacturer of heavy industrial equipment.

At some companies, a stockholders meeting is treated as an important communications discipline for the officers and directors of the corporation. Once a year top management must come forward to a public platform and provide an accounting of its stewardship. At the same time, the officers are exposed to inquiries ranging from those of the business reporter to the uninformed questions of Aunt Jane, and from the annoying question of a dissident to the perceptive question of a financial analyst. This is one opportunity, and perhaps the only one, for managers to discover what a varied audience may think about their performance and the company as an investment entity, corporate citizen, or employer. Some companies are known to welcome the presence of such well-known "professional" stockholders as Lewis and John Gilbert, who continually pressure management with their critical questions on cumulative voting rights for stockholders, staggered elections of directors, and a host of other small-stockholder concerns. Thus, for both the individual stockholder and corporate manager, the meeting may provide a safety valve, where once a year problems and complaints ranging from dividend dissatisfaction to the intricacies of a tender offer or proxy fight are placed in the public arena for resolution.

Among corporations with large stockholder populations spread throughout the United States, regional meetings have been organized by managements seeking more personal contact and communication with shareholders. General Electric has used an alternating method by holding the meeting required by state law in one six-month period and an informational-type meeting in a different part of the country in the next six-month period. Television may be utilized to include more stockholders. Eastman Kodak has held a morning business meeting for stockholders in New Jersey, its state of incorporation, then moved the meeting to its home base of Rochester, New York, for an evening televised meeting at which stockholders could telephone the television station to have questions answered by management. A number of other companies have varied their annual meeting location or have held quarterly informational meetings in cities where sizable numbers of stockholders are concentrated.

A management that is concerned about the ownership participation of the small investor will often encourage an active annual meeting agenda. Regardless of the size of individual holdings of those present, whether attendees are retired or active, or whether attendance is large or small, these corporate officers feel a real obligation and a need to communicate to the average shareholder. Their annual meeting is treated with the same reverence as a New England town hall meeting. Even if the shareholder leaves the meeting with no altered or informed impression of the proceedings of the company, he feels a worthwhile exercise in corporate democracy has been performed. Moreover, a degree of stockholder loyalty may be developed that can be translated into tangible results at some later occasion—perhaps when the company requires additional financing or management needs a vote of confidence for some future proposal.

AN AREA OF DISENCHANTMENT

Given the number of very real benefits that can be realized from a commitment to annual meetings, why is it that such a large and increasingly vocal number of corporate executives have decided to discourage, downplay, and even avoid the function at a time when corporate disclosure practices are a major concern? Unfortunately, not all managements believe that widely disseminated corporate information is the best policy to follow. They see their communications program as a carefully controlled way of saying the least possible about company operations. A related management practice may be to take a positive communications approach only when earnings are trending upward, but to withdraw when profits are in decline. The annual meeting could be the first casualty in this type of policy. Only legal requirements and the fear of criticism from shareholders, consumer groups, and other interested parties force some managements to continue the exercise.

For many companies, the state of incorporation that calls for an annual meeting is not the corporate headquarters, or even a center of stockholder concentration. This may serve as a convenient reason to downgrade the practice. In fact, avoidance of a large gathering of stockholders may be the major factor in a company's incorporating away from the home base of operations, or it may be a corollary benefit for noncommunicative management.

Often the lack of interest in communications on management's part is reinforced by stockholder apathy. One of the sharpest criticisms of annual meetings is that attendance is poor when compared with the total stockholder population, or even that of the state or city in which the meeting is held. For most companies the number of attendees at a meeting is well under one percent of the total number of stockholders. Management understandably questions whether an all-out effort is worth the commitment of considerable time and expense.

Why don't stockholders attend annual meetings in greater numbers? A major factor is the national and international distribution of many firms' stockholder population. It simply isn't practical or necessary to travel to an annual meeting when voting prerogatives can be exercised with a proxy. A less obvious reason is that the majority of stockholders purchase their shares on the recommendation of a stockbroker. The decision to buy more shares or to sell existing shares is not influenced by annual meeting participation. Also, the number of stockholders holding shares in brokerage street name has increased greatly in the past decade. Such a situation is not conducive to annual meeting participation.

Another attendance factor is that annual meetings have developed a reputation for dullness. Not only stockholders but the business and financial media, financial analysts, employees, and other supposedly interested parties have been conditioned by the belief that nothing of real significance transpires at the average corporate stockholder gathering. Therefore, why devote valuable time to a mechanical exercise? With a corporate ego bruised by a poor showing, a negative attitude toward meetings may consciously or unconsciously prevail. Management feels the annual meeting is poorly attended and so devotes less energy in making it an attractive and meaningful investor relations vehicle.

Perhaps the strongest motivation for a management to downplay the annual meeting is the reaction to a new consideration in corporate life—organized dissent. This is not the familiar and frequently constructive prodding of the "professional" stockholders, but the social, environmental, and consumer activists who have begun to use the annual meeting as a platform for protest and pressure. After long histories of somnolent stockholder gatherings, many executives now find protest groups have added an extra dimension to their stockholder event of the year.

THE ANNUAL MEETING IN THE 1970s

"For the most part, annual meetings will be largely routine affairs in which the most pressing business will be to terminate the meeting." *

By the opening months of the 1970s, there were already profound changes in the structure, the handling, and indeed the very concept of what the annual meeting was supposed to be. The changes were perpetrated largely by outside forces, but they required a new kind of response from management. The annual meeting became a public platform for the airing of a whole range of social, environmental, racial, minority, and other causes that heretofore had been regarded as simply not the business of the corporation in American·society. The transformation of the annual meeting into an arena of vocal if not angry protest was not accidental, but coincidental—coincidental with widening public interest in and impatience with the apparent indifference of established centers of power and authority in our society toward the broad social issues of the day.

Certainly it is true that only a very small percentage of American corporations was directly involved in these early confrontations, and they tended to be large companies with defense contracts or companies whose business operations created or affected environmental problems. But a wide variety of other issues, some of them seemingly unrelated to the business of the company, surfaced in the form of stockholder protest. Many managements were forced to

* *Business Week,* April 6, 1968.

acknowledge that the annual meeting wasn't the routine affair it used to be, and what happened to a Dow Chemical Company or Honeywell or Consolidated Edison could happen to the smaller, lesser-known company if the right issues and determined proponents got together.

For people involved in investor relations, the question is not so much "How do we develop a battle plan?" as, more pragmatically, "What do we need to know about the handling of stockholder participation in our annual meeting?"

The first step is to determine the kind of stockholder you are dealing with. There are important differences in intent and objectives. A simplified delineation might be: (1) the serious stockholder with a legitimate concern about what the company is doing or how it is being managed—issues which, in his opinion, affect his decision as to whether he wishes to continue to hold stock in the company; (2) the "professional" stockholder whose traditional recommendations may be legitimately related to the business of the annual meeting; and (3) the agitator, who increasingly is trained in the skills of intervention, disruption, confrontation, and sustained dissidence.

Essential to an understanding of the situation is to know what the respective rights of both stockholders and management are and how to run the annual meeting on behalf of the majority interest in a fair yet firm manner.

The American Society of Corporate Secretaries, Inc., located in New York City, has prepared several manuals, one dealing with the preparations and procedures of stockholder meetings and two on how to conduct annual meetings. The manuals cover both the mechanics of a routine annual meeting and strategies and suggestions for handling unusual or special situations. In addition, the SEC has updated some pertinent guidelines on proxy materials which can be found in Release No. 34-9784 ("Adoption of Amendments to Proxy Rules") and Release No. 34-9785 ("Adoption of Section 200.82 Concerning Public Availability of Materials Filed Pursuant to Proxy Rule 14a-8(d) and Related Materials"), both dated September 22, 1972.

Briefly, according to the established procedure for stockholder proposals, any stockholder may submit to management in writing and before a specified deadline one or more proposals and their supporting statements, to be included with the proxy form and proxy materials sent by management to all stockholders of a specified record date. Management may agree or decline to include such proposals but must, again within a specified time period, advise the SEC of the proposals, management's decision about them, and the reasons for it. The SEC may uphold or differ with that decision and order management to include one or more proposals as proper to the business of the annual meeting. If the SEC upholds management's decision to exclude proposals, the proposers may appeal to a court of law. The SEC has commented on the nature and extent of acceptable stockholder proposals and expanded the time limits for their submission, review, and appeal. It is also clear that the SEC expects stockholders to be present at the annual meeting to present their proposals, and it has made several general pronouncements all basically designed to provide somewhat better control, for both management's and stockholders' benefit, over the whole proposal procedure.

Whether proposals can be made by stockholders or proxyholders from the floor is a procedural decision that management can make and announce at the opening of the meeting. If management is opposed to a floor proposal, it has only to let it be placed in motion for vote. Since any proposal, whether from the floor or included in the proxy material, must have a majority of all votes present to pass, including those signed over to management, the results are usually predictable. Most companies seem to be coming to the conclusion that it is easier, though certainly not less costly in time and expense, to include a reasonable number of stockholder proposals in proxy material and advise against those to which they are opposed. However, under SEC rules, any proposal that receives 3 percent or more of the vote can be resubmitted the following year and does not have to wait the customary three years required for those that get less than 3 percent.

A study of 654 member companies compiled in 1970 by the American Society of Corporate Secretaries found that an average of only 11 percent of those companies received proposals from stockholders for inclusion in proxy material; an average of only 9 percent were opposed by management; and only 5 percent reported that an organized group had ever acted at one of their annual meetings. The percentage in each category was significantly higher in companies with large numbers of stockholders, indicating that protest has been aimed at fairly specific and sizable target companies in the early part of the decade.

Protest, at least large-scale disruptive protest, may prove to be neither a fad nor a campaign, but a phenomenon that ran its course along with campus turmoil, antiwar movements, and other developments that shared in their tactics some common characteristics. The consensus among investor relations specialists is that stockholder protest won't fade away. Rather, it will become more sophisticated and sharper edged and be handled by "public interest" lawyers.

Certainly anyone involved in investor relations recognizes the power of the collective stockholder body. Proper resolutions, well publicized and adopted, often through support from the holdings of schools, universities, and churches, have been surprisingly effective in bringing about corporate policy changes.

CONTROLLING ATTENDANCE

Annual meetings have been open, or public, meetings only as a result of management choice and past practice. As a matter of law, annual meetings are in fact private meetings, and the only people entitled to be there are the stockholders of the specified record date, their duly appointed proxies, and invited guests, such as media representatives and security analysts. Annual meetings by law are not public forums for anything, social issues or otherwise. But because of the changed nature of the annual meeting for some companies, the issue of attendance has, probably for the first time, become just that—an issue.

Many companies now limit admission to the groups named above and employ a variety of different ways to do this. They may require an advance reservation from the stockholder or proxyholder in response to which the company sends an admission ticket or other form of entrance card. Or they may check off each person against stockholder lists at the entrance to the meeting, with a separate table set up to handle proxyholders. Another procedure is to have each person sign a register or identification card (more as a record of attendance than a control).

One of the major difficulties in controlling admission is that neither state corporation laws nor the SEC has yet developed any specific rules or guidelines on the number of proxies any one stockholder may appoint to represent him. Companies that have faced this problem have had little recourse but to make up their own rules on the number they will admit.* They have faced some trying situations as a result.

THE CONTENT OF THE MEETING

In the routine annual meeting, the typical three items of business presented for vote on the proxy and at the meeting are the election of directors, the selection of an auditor, and "any other business which might come before the meeting" —but rarely does. The first two, along with stockholder approval of certain acquisitions and stockholder authorization for additional equity issues, are the only items of business required by law to be presented and voted on, including the proxy votes, at an annual meeting.

For many companies this agenda hasn't changed and probably won't change significantly. But for a good number of corporations, some advance and simultaneous new steps have become necessary. Among these are:

Establishing rules of subject matter. This pertains once again to the question and problem of relevant and appropriate stockholder proposals and other forms of participation in the meeting. Management can and should make a simple statement at the opening of the meeting about what it feels constitutes relevant subject matter.

Establishing rules of behavior. This is part of the same situation, and again requires an opening statement by management as to what time limits will be allowed each speaker, how many times one person may speak, and so forth.

* "Handling Protest at Annual Meetings," The Conference Board, New York, 1971.

Enforcement and security measures. Some preparation may be necessary to insure that the meeting proceeds without monopoly by any one stockholder or more or that actual disruption is not permitted. This may be as simple as controlling the placement and volume of the microphones in the room or as complex as switching to an abbreviated agenda in order to conclude the business and adjourn the meeting. Disruptive stockholders and proxyholders can be evicted from the meeting on grounds that relate to the property rights of management to control the premises.

Some companies have gone so far as to develop evacuation routes for executives, bomb-threat response plans, and other procedures to handle emergency situations. By and large, the most widely made change has been to alter the agenda so that any sensitive area of business is held for discussion and vote until the required items have been covered, allowing for an early adjournment but still complying with the law.

THE CONSENT PROCEDURE AND THE FUTURE OF THE ANNUAL MEETING

In mid-1969, the state of Delaware changed its laws to permit companies incorporated there to use a consent vote procedure and thus eliminate the actual physical gathering of a stockholder meeting. Since Delaware is the state of incorporation for a significant number of American corporations and since other states are following Delaware's lead, holding the annual meeting could become a matter of choice rather than necessity.

The principle of the consent method is that of direct balloting by stockholders by mail on those items of business requiring stockholder approval or authorization. The procedure generally involves two steps: (1) solicitation by management of stockholder approval to change existing corporate bylaws that require the annual meeting to be the focal point of ownership representation, and (2) subsequent or simultaneous direct solicitation by mail of stockholder votes for directors and on other matters that would traditionally come before an annual meeting.

A simple majority (50 percent plus one of total shares outstanding) is needed both to gain approval of this direct vote method and to pass on regular management proposals.

Under most statutory requirements governing the traditional procedures, a defined number or quorum of shares must be represented in person or signed over to management to conduct the meeting, and a simple majority of those voting shares is necessary to execute standard business. Action can be taken by a relatively small percent of total shares and stockholder population. One midwestern state requires voting representation of one-third of total outstanding shares, with a simple majority necessary for action. Thus it is possible that little more than one-sixth of the total shares could swing the vote.

Probably the leading proponent of the consent method is J. B. Fuqua, chairman of Fuqua Industries, quoted in the opening of this article. His views and arguments for the consent vote and against the annual meeting highlight the alleged weaknesses of the traditional vehicle and have received considerable national attention. A paraphrase of those arguments might be this:

> The annual meeting is anything but an exercise in stockholder democracy. The voting structure is based on economic power: votes are bought by buying shares.

Actual attendance never approaches a democratic representation of the majority, which has in practice already decided the vote by signing proxies over to management.

Street-name and broker-nominee shares often aren't voted; institutions and funds, where involved, usually swing the vote.

Stronger disclosure requirements of the SEC and stock exchanges calling for the prompt, simultaneous release of material information throughout the year downgrade the annual meeting as an "exclusive" news vehicle.

Most security analysts and professional investors prefer to contact the company directly and don't rely on the annual meeting for significant information.

The annual meeting has become a platform for individuals and groups who want to use it for personal publicity or to promulgate some cause.

The time and expense devoted by management to the annual meeting go beyond necessity and are all out of proportion to the usefulness of the meeting.

At the 1972 annual meeting, Fuqua management proposed a new bylaw to drop its meeting and have future participation by mailed ballot. The proposal carried by the largest affirmative stockholder vote in the company's history.

The Fuqua effort drew a strong response from others concerned about the effectiveness of their annual meetings. So much so that in early 1973 the New York Stock Exchange recognized the validity of the consent method to transact stockholder business, provided the following requirements were met:

A stockholder record date must be used.

Consent material must be sent to all shareholders.

Corporate action is not to be taken until the solicitation period has expired, even if the required vote is received earlier.

A thirty-day solicitation period is recommended, with a period of twenty days required.

Consent material should conform to normal proxy disclosure standards.

The Exchange still views an actual meeting of shareholders as a necessary exercise in corporate democracy and candid self-appraisal for management. But with the use of the consent method for transacting legal business, the meetings will become informational in nature.

Such official policy changes will be slow in coming, since the arguments over annual meetings are based on feelings and convictions that are not likely to be quickly altered. The prognosis is probably that the annual meeting will continue to survive in some form. Whether it is in fact the most important investor relations event of the year is a question that only individual company managements can decide.

Investor Relations
and the Law

William H. Dinsmore

THE LAW is constantly changing, and the investor relations professional is thus faced with a continuing need to educate and update himself. It is an encouraging fact, however, that good investor relations practice has always been ahead of the law. Frequently the new law has been developed in the courts on a case-by-case basis and what was not formerly a legal requirement may become so ex post facto. Therefore, to insure that investor relations–related activities do not run afoul of the law, the safest course is always what seems sound and ethical in accordance with the best investor relations experience, whether or not it is proscribed or prescribed by law.

Some people trace the lineage of today's investor relations law back to the English Bubble Act of 1720. It was enacted by Parliament after thousands saw their life savings

William H. Dinsmore is President, William H. Dinsmore Associates, New York, N.Y.

vanish when shares of the South Seas Company (with George I as its governor) tumbled from £1,000 in July to £125 in December. After the debacle, outraged "little investors" learned that directors of the company had sold shares for five million at the top.

In the United States the earliest efforts at securities regulation began at the state level. Professor Louis Loss, author of the authoritative textbook on securities regulation, cites the Massachusetts statute of 1852, which provided:

> No railroad company hereafter charted in this Commonwealth, shall begin to build its road until a certificate shall have been filed in the office of the secretary of the Commonwealth . . . stating that all of the stock named in the charter has been subscribed for by responsible parties, and that twenty per cent of the par value of each and every share of the stock thereof has been actually paid into the treasury of the company.*

But the disclosure philosophy that underlies both the federal and many of the states' securities laws today traces its origins to the English Companies Act of 1900. It was based on a committee report which deemed it

> of the highest importance that the prospectus upon which the public are invited to subscribe shall not only not contain any misrepresentation but shall satisfy a high standard of good faith. It may be a counsel of perfection and impossible of attainment to say that a prospectus shall disclose everything which could reasonably influence the mind of an investor of average prudence. But this in the opinion of your Committee is the ideal to be aimed at.

---

* *Securities Regulation* (Boston: Little, Brown and Company), 1961, p. 23.

This philosophy of disclosure was expressed by President Roosevelt in his message to Congress of March 29, 1933:

> Of course, the Federal Government cannot and should not take any action which might be construed as approving or guaranteeing that newly issued securities are sound in the sense that their value will be maintained or that the properties which they represent will earn profit.
>
> There is, however, an obligation upon us to insist that every issue of new securities to be sold in interstate commerce shall be accompanied by full publicity and information, and no essentially important element attending the issue will be concealed from the buying public.
>
> This proposal adds to the ancient rule of caveat emptor, the further doctrine "let the seller also beware." It puts the burden of telling the whole truth on the seller. It should give impetus to honest dealing in securities and thereby bring back public confidence.

The resulting Securities Act of 1933 is concerned largely with the initial distribution of securities rather than trading. But it also established what has been described as the "keystone of the entire structure of securities legislation . . . disclosure." In its 1934 report on stock exchange practices, the Senate Committee on Banking and Currency stated:

> It is universally conceded that adequate information as to the financial structure and condition of a corporation is indispensable to an intelligent determination of the quality of its securities. The concept of a free and open market for securities necessarily implies that the buyer and seller are acting in the exercise of enlightened judgment as to what constitutes a fair price. Insofar as the judgment is warped by false, inaccurate, or incomplete information regarding

the corporation, the market place fails to reflect the normal operation of supply and demand. One of the prime concerns of the exchanges should be to make available to the public honest, complete and accurate information regarding the securities listed.

The 1933 Act was at first administered by the Federal Trade Commission. The Securities and Exchange Commission was established by the Securities Exchange Act of 1934, which extended the disclosure philosophy to trading in all securities listed on the exchanges. It had four basic purposes: to make disclosure available to people who buy and sell securities; to prevent fraud in securities trading, and manipulation of the market; to regulate the securities markets; and to control the amount of the nation's credit that goes into those markets.

The SEC was given administrative responsibility for both the 1933 and 1934 acts and subsequently for the Public Utility Holding Company Act of 1935, the Trust Indenture Act of 1939, the Investment Company Act of 1940, and the Investment Advisers Act of 1940. It also has advisory functions in corporate reorganization proceedings under Chapter X of the Bankruptcy Act.

Under the 1933 Act, most new issues of securities offered to the public by mail or other channels of interstate commerce must be registered with the SEC, and a prospectus containing financial and other material information must be furnished to the purchaser. The act applies whether or not the securities are part of an issue listed on an exchange. For listed securities, the 1934 Act provided additional safeguards in sections 12, 13, 14, and 16, which rely on the principles of disclosure and self-protection. As a prerequisite to listing, Section 12 requires filing with both the exchange involved and the SEC a registration statement similar to that required for new issues. Section 13 requires that this information be kept up to date by annual and other periodic reports. Regulations currently provide for the filing of the following reports:

Annual report (Form 10-K). Required data include description of principal products and services and—"if applicable and material for an understanding of the business" —competitive conditions in the industry; dollar amount of backlog of orders; the source and availability of raw material; all material patents, licenses, franchises, and concessions; estimated dollar amount spent on material research activities; number of employees; sales and revenues for the last five years of principal lines of business; description of principal physical properties; list or diagram of parents and subsidiaries; pending legal proceedings; changes in outstanding securities; principal holders of voting securities; name, principal occupation, and shareholdings of directors; remuneration, including amounts accrued in retirement plans, of each director and principal officer; stock options outstanding and the exercise of options; any interest of an officer or director in a material transaction of the corporation; and financial statements prepared in accordance with the Commission's accounting regulations and certified by an independent public accountant. Form 10-K must be filed with the SEC and exchanges where listed no later than ninety days after the close of the fiscal year.

Quarterly reports (Form 10-Q). Required data for the first three quarters include summarized profit and loss information, capitalization and stockholders' equity as of the end of the quarter, and sales of unregistered securities. The form must be filed within forty-five days after the end of the quarter.

Current report (Form 8-K). Filing is required on the occurrence of an unusual event of immediate interest to investors, for example, changes in control of the issuer; acquisition or sale of a significant amount of assets; changes in amount of securities outstanding and any change in the rights of security holders, including any defaults upon senior securities and the issuance of new options; the institution of material legal proceedings; and any matter that requires a vote of security holders.

Section 14 and SEC regulations under it govern the form, content, and manner of solicitation of proxies relating to listed securities to provide stockholders with accurate and adequate information on which to base their votes.

Proxy statements must include information about the persons on whose behalf the proxies are solicited, nominees for directorships, and other matters to be voted on. When management of a listed company solicits proxies, the statement must also include information on management compensation, including bonuses, pensions and profit-sharing plans, loans to directors and officers, and material transactions between the corporation and its officers, directors, and principal shareholders. If the proxy relates to a meeting at which directors are to be selected, the shareholders must be supplied with an annual report containing such information as will, in the opinion of management, adequately reflect the financial position and operations of the company. Although not originally legally required, the SEC and others increasingly urge that the annual report to shareholders include all material information that is reported in the 10-K form filed with the SEC.

Section 16 of the 1934 Act is aimed at preventing short-swing trading profits by "insiders." Section 16(a) requires each officer, director, and beneficial owner of more than

10 percent of any listed class of equity security to file with the SEC and the exchange an initial statement of his holdings and monthly reports (Form 4) reflecting any changes in his holdings. Section 16(b) provides for the recovery, by or on behalf of a corporation, of all profits realized by an insider from a purchase or sale of the corporation's stock within any period of less than six months. Section 16(c) forbids short-selling by insiders, or selling shares and failing to deliver certificates within twenty days after the sale.

Statutory protections afforded investors are supplemented by controls exercised over the issuers by listing agreements with the exchanges. The New York and American Stock exchanges require all listed companies to issue to shareholders annual, independently audited financial statements and to submit copies to newspapers, wire services, and statistical services.

Both the major exchanges have policies and guidelines for timely disclosure of information that go beyond the statutory requirements, and it is necessary to study carefully both the listing agreements and the specific policies set forth in their disclosure manuals (see the appendix "Policies and Guidelines of the Major Stock Exchanges"). One of the most important provisions is the "telephone alert" procedure requiring listed companies to notify the exchange when a material disclosure is being made during or shortly before trading hours. By receiving the information no later than the news media, the exchange is able to evaluate whether trading should be temporarily stopped pending public evaluation of the information released.

The disclosure policy of the exchanges in respect to rumors that result in unusual market activity or price variation may well have given rise to the *Texas Gulf Sulphur* case, which will be discussed in more detail later. Texas

Gulf was under no statutory obligation to issue the now-famous news release of April 12, 1964. Part of the company's defense was that this was a cautionary "wait and see" release required by the NYSE to "act promptly to dispel unfounded rumors which result in unusual market activity or price variation. . . . If rumors are in fact false or inaccurate, they should be promptly denied or clarified."

In 1964, Congress amended the 1934 Act to extend to many of the over-the-counter stocks (corporations with assets of a million dollars and five hundred or more stockholders) disclosure requirements that formerly applied only to securities listed on the exchanges. The amendments stemmed from the 1962 Special Study of the Securities Markets of the SEC. Its findings and recommendations were reported in a three-volume, three-thousand-page report to Congress in 1963.

The Special Study found that on the whole the 1933 and 1934 acts had worked well over a period of more than twenty-five years in achieving the objectives of full and fair disclosure and greater stability in the markets. It also quoted with approval the finding of Dr. Corliss Anderson in a study of corporate reporting sponsored by the Financial Analysts Federation. Dr. Anderson's statement reflected what many investor relations professionals would regard as sound policy, irrespective of the law:

> We believe that no responsible management wants to have among its shareholders those who have paid too much for the stock of their company due to inadequate or poorly timed information.
>
> Unfounded rumors grow better in darkness than in the light of facts. The policy of providing complete information at the usual periodic reporting times has the definite advantage of precluding great "surprises" to the share-

holders and, perhaps more importantly, it lessens the likelihood of excessive overevaluation or underevaluation of the company's common stocks in the marketplace.

The Special Study group suggested that this principle applied with even greater urgency to the lesser-known companies whose stocks were not listed on the exchanges.

The Special Study report also included the first comprehensive study of financial public relations practices. It noted that informal corporate publicity was an important supplement to the disclosures required by the 1933 and 1934 acts and was in fact affirmatively encouraged by the SEC's Release No. 3844 of 1957, which said in part:

> There has been an increasing tendency, particularly in the period since World War II, to give publicity through many media concerning corporate affairs which goes beyond the statutory requirements. This practice reflects a commendable and growing recognition on the part of industry and the investment community of the importance of informing security holders and the public generally with respect to important business and financial developments. This trend should be encouraged.

Nevertheless, the report said, the Commission and its staff had recently become aware, particularly during a speculative bull market, "of disturbing signs that public relations consultants and corporate public relations departments have been used for purposes contrary to the letter and spirit of the securities acts."

Most of the forty-odd pages of this section of the study were devoted to a recitation of dubious case histories, the most notable of which involved not a public relations practitioner but a former business news editor of *Time* magazine who had on many occasions invested in the stock of a little-known company just before publishing a lead article about some new development in the company. Other examples included "inaccurate and irresponsible corporate publicity" concerning the success of the BarChris Construction Corporation's bowling alley ventures in Europe; several companies whose publicity gave out "sales and earnings estimates that turned out to be too high"; and "overenthusiastic and premature publicity concerning product developments."

While the study concluded that there should be "a statute designed to prevent misuse of channels of publicity [which] should provide for both civil and criminal sanctions," it also acknowledged that "there are limits to what can and should be accomplished by direct regulation in this area." It added:

> The volume of corporate publicity, the paramount aim of full and prompt disclosure, the difficulty of making judgments concerning specific items of publicity, and the proximity of this field to the constitutionally protected right of freedom of expression—all combine to make legal control a relatively clumsy instrument.

Prophetically, the Special Study noted in 1962 that a "body of case law has developed which indicates that Rule 10b-5 may provide a remedy to investors who buy or sell securities on the basis of false information disseminated by corporate officials or their publicity agents." While the study noted certain limitations in the application of Rule 10b-5, subsequent developments, notably the *SEC–Texas Gulf Sulphur* case, rapidly removed the limitations during the balance of the decade.

Rule 10b-5 makes it unlawful "to make any untrue statement of a material fact or to omit to state a material fact necessary in order to make the statement made, in the light of the circumstances under which [it was] made, not misleading . . . in connection with the purchase or sale of any security." The rule was adopted by the SEC in 1942 in response to a case wherein, according to its author:

> The president of some company in Boston is going around buying up the stock of his company from his own shareholders at $4.00 a share, and he has been telling them that the company is doing very badly, whereas, in fact, the earnings are going to be quadrupled and will be $2.00 for this coming year.

SEC Release No. 3280 (May 21, 1942) announced, "The new rule closes a loophole in the protections against fraud by the Commission by prohibiting individuals or companies from buying securities if they engage in fraud in their purchase."

The *Texas Gulf* case brought by the SEC in April 1965 was the first to assert that a company press release violated Rule 10b-5, even though it was not made in connection with the purchase or sale of stock. The SEC charged that the company's press release of April 12, 1964, commenting on rumors of a major ore find near Timmins, Ontario, was materially false and misleading. The question of whether the facts known in the early stages of Texas Gulf's exploration were "material" became a key issue. At the initial trial, the SEC proposed two tests of materiality:

> First, it is a fact of which a reasonably prudent investor would wish to be informed before making a decision to buy or sell, or alternatively it is a fact the disclosure of which can reasonably be anticipated to have significant impact upon the market for the security involved. A fact which would be material in the affairs of one company

would probably not be material in the affairs of another, depending upon the relative size and financial condition of the enterprise and the nature of their business and the market for their securities.

After a lengthy trial in Federal District Court in 1966, Judge Dudley B. Bonsal found that the results of the first drill hole were "too 'remote' when considered in the light of the size of TGS, the scope of its activities, and the number of outstanding shares, to have had any significant impact on the market, i.e., to be deemed material." He also found that the results of a second hole drilled five months later in April 1964 "did not constitute material information. If disclosed it would not have had a substantial impact on the market price of the company's stock."

On the basis of these findings, the trial court dismissed the SEC's complaint against the company and most of the individual defendants. Appealing, the SEC said, "There is no justification for the district judge's view that 'information is not material merely because it would be of interest to the speculator on Bay Street or Wall Street.'" After seventeen months of deliberation, the U.S. Court of Appeals for the Second Circuit agreed and held in August 1968 that "the speculators and chartists of Wall and Bay Streets are also 'reasonable' investors . . . ," and that "material facts include . . . those which may affect the desire of investors to buy, sell, or hold the company's securities."

In the evolution of Rule 10b-5 two cases are often cited which bracketed the *Texas Gulf* case in time, although both of these were administrative proceedings that never reached the courts. In the *Cady, Roberts* case in 1961, the SEC charged that the registered representative of a brokerage firm who was also a director of Curtiss-Wright had telephoned news of a dividend cut to a partner in his firm before the announcement had been made public. According to the SEC, the partner violated Rule 10b-5 when he sold Curtiss-Wright shares on the basis of what he knew was undisclosed material information. Further, this case made amply clear the "inherent unfairness" involved in a person's taking advantage of such information knowing it is unavailable to those with whom he is dealing. The *Merrill Lynch* case followed quickly on the heels of the circuit court opinion in *Texas Gulf*. The SEC charged that the world's largest brokerage firm, fourteen of its senior employees, and fourteen institutional investors violated Rule 10b-5 in connection with the stock of the Douglas Aircraft Company. The SEC said that in mid-1966 Merrill Lynch passed along information about Douglas' poor earnings outlook to the institutions—information it got while acting as underwriter for a Douglas debenture issue. The SEC charged that the institutions sold Douglas shares, or sold Douglas short, before the public knew about the poor earnings. When the news was made public, Douglas shares plunged.

While *Cady, Roberts* and *Merrill Lynch* may be important cases for establishing new standards of fair dealing in the brokerage community, neither seems to involve any ambiguity for a corporate communicator in respect to the materiality of the facts involved. In a sequel to *Merrill Lynch,* however, the SEC on July 29, 1971, made an effort to spell out in further detail the factors to be considered in determining materiality. Holding that censure was an appropriate penalty in the *Investors Management Co., Inc., et al.* case (the institutions charged in the *Merrill Lynch* case), the SEC said:

With respect to materiality, we held in our findings with regard to Merrill Lynch in these proceedings that the information as to Douglas' earnings that it divulged was material because it "was of such importance that it could be expected to affect the judgment of investors whether to buy, sell, or hold Douglas stock [and if] generally known . . . to affect materially the market price of the stock."

Among the factors to be considered in determining whether information is material under this test are the degree of its specificity, the extent to which it differs from information previously publicly disseminated and its reliability in light of its nature and source and the circumstances under which it was received.

While the test would not embrace information as to minor aspects or routine details of a company's operations, the information received by the respondents was highly significant since it described a sharp reversal of Douglas' earnings realization and expectations.

The corporate communicator's most difficult task in complying with investor relations law may be the exercise of sound judgment in determining the how and when of disclosure of material facts. The dilemma is well expressed by Professor Alan R. Bromberg, author of McGraw-Hill's authoritative textbook on Rule 10b-5, who commented that "including speculators among the reasonable investors used for the measure of materiality" has further stretched the meaning of the term. He added, "In view of the way market professionals sometimes react to relatively slight bits of information, the court's standard seems to set a regrettably low threshold of materiality." *

In Professor Bromberg's view, however, even more important than any particular holding in the *Texas Gulf* case

* *Securities Laws: Fraud—SEC Rule 10b-5, 1969, Sec. 7.4(3)(c),* p. 168.4.

is the court's enunciation of an underlying philosophy of insuring that equality of information is available to all investors:

> It is an egalitarian idea expressed several times in similar phrases. In general, it is that all investors shall "have relatively equal access to material information." Relative to nondisclosure (by insiders trading with material information), it is that "all investors should have equal access to the rewards of participation in securities transactions . . . and be subject to identical market risks." (The court recognizes that these "risks include, of course, the risk that one's evaluative capacity or one's capital available to put at risk may exceed another's capacity or capital.") In deciding whether the press release was "in connection with" a securities transaction the court stated that the purpose of federal securities law is "to protect the investing public from suffering inequities in trading, including, specifically, inequities that follow from trading that has been stimulated by the publication of false or misleading corporate information releases."

Although the SEC has resisted adopting more specific guidelines for measuring materiality, arguing that each case must be judged on its merits, it has in recent years issued releases attempting to clarify areas of information where the need for prompt disclosure of a corporate development should be considered in fairness to the investing public as well as stockholders. Some of these areas are:

Earnings, including comparisons with similar periods for the prior year and information with respect to the comparability of the figures given.

Financing, including the issuance of new securities or the floating of new debt.

Acquisitions and divestitures. The timing of announcement is critical. The NYSE policy requires disclosure as soon as confidential details become available to those other than top management and their "individual confidential advisers."

New products or discoveries. Here again the timing as to when the information becomes "material" is a critical matter for judgment.

Personnel changes, normally including officers and directors, but which may include key personnel, such as well-known scientists, major plant closings, or employee layoffs.

Write-offs. Major accounting write-offs should be disclosed as soon as corporate decisions have definitely been made and not delayed until formal action by auditors at year's end.

Litigation, which may include threatened litigation or claims that require disclosure because of materiality. SEC spokesmen have recently included environmental requirements as an area of concern.

Cash-flow and other liquidity problems. Prompt disclosure may be necessary even though, because of the timing, the disclosure itself might handicap the company's efforts to solve the problems involved.

The SEC has also emphasized the importance of promptly disclosing the bad news along with the good. Following the Penn Central debacle, the Commission issued Securities Act Release No. 5092 on October 15, 1970, in which it reiterated the "need for publicly held companies to make prompt and accurate disclosure of information, both favorable and unfavorable, to security holders and the investing public." The release stressed that even when a company has made timely filing of all periodic reports required by the 1934 Act or the Investment Company Act, "it still has an obligation to make full and prompt announcements of material facts regarding the company's financial condition."

The responsibility rests with company managements, which have intimate knowledge

> of factors affecting profits and losses, such as curtailment of operations, decline of orders, or cost overruns on major contracts. They are also cognizant of liquidity problems, such as decreased inflow collections from sales to customers, the availability or lack of availability of credit from suppliers, banks, and other financial institutions, and the inability to meet maturing obligations when they fall due. Managements of registered investment companies are similarly aware of such factors affecting the operations of the business of such companies as changes in important personnel of the company or its investment adviser, insolvency of such an adviser or the investment company's principal underwriter, or inability of an investment adviser to meet an expense guarantee or make a performance fee refund to the company.
>
> Not only must material facts affecting the company's operations be reported; they must also be reported promptly. Corporate releases which disclose personnel changes, the receipt of new contracts, orders and other favorable developments, but do not even suggest existing adverse corporate developments do not serve the public needs and may violate the anti-fraud provisions [of the 1934 Act and, during an offering of shares, the 1933 Act] if the prospectus is not appropriately updated.

The release referred to the prompt disclosure policies of the exchanges and added the warning that "unless adequate and accurate information is available, a company may not be able to purchase its own securities or make acquisitions using its securities, and insiders may not be able to trade its securities without running serious risk of violating" Rule 10b-5.

Under Chairman William J. Casey, the SEC reexamined its long-standing policies regarding disclosure of economic forecasts. Traditionally, projections of sales and earnings were prohibited in registration statements under the 1933 and 1934 acts.

"There are many who feel that forecasting can be misleading, can create new problems and new liabilities," Casey has said. "We share those concerns, but it is not a simple choice between exposure to liability and freedom from liability or between forecasts and no forecasts. We have forecasts, they are in circulation, they are sometimes misleading and can always affect stock values."

Casey cited, with approval, a 1971 decision (*Dolgow* v. *Anderson*) in the Federal District Court for the Eastern District of New York that protected officers and directors of the Monsanto Company against private suits for liability on grounds that their earnings-forecast program had been carried out in good faith.

In the broadest sense of investor relations and the law, the greater significance of *Dolgow* v. *Anderson* was Monsanto's ability to demonstrate to the court that the company had over a period of years consistently followed "a broad program for advising its shareholders and the public at large of the results of past operations, of future prospects and of current developments and problems." Judge Jack B. Weinstein's opinion (*Federal Securities Law Reporter,* CCH ¶93,249) is worth close study by all those concerned with the overall corporate investor relations policy and program.

Meeting
with Security Analysts

Charles L. Cohen

In its company manual, the New York Stock Exchange
defines relationships that should exist between company
officials and security analysts as follows:

> Security analysts play an increasingly important role
> in the evaluation and interpretation of the financial affairs
> of listed companies. Annual reports, quarterly reports, and
> interim releases cannot by their nature provide all of the
> financial and statistical data that should be available to the
> investing public. The Exchange recommends that cor-
> porations observe an "open door" policy in their relations
> with security analysts, financial writers, shareowners, and
> others who have a legitimate investment interest in the
> company's affairs.

Other exchanges have similar regulations, and the Securities and Exchange Commission has consistently encour-

Charles L. Cohen is Director, Investor Relations, Lear Siegler, Inc.,
Santa Monica, Calif.

aged corporations to maintain continuing and meaningful relationships with security analysts.

There is more involved in meeting with security analysts than merely observing protocol. The very health of securities markets and of business itself depends upon a continuing flow of comprehensible, consistent, and accurate information to all segments of the investing public. The flow of such information is in turn dependent upon relationships that have been established between security analysts and investor relations executives.

The analyst is continually evaluating corporate activities, programs, plans, and concepts. He is making judgments as to the worth of corporate securities under a variety of situations and circumstances. The analyst's counterpart, the investor relations executive, is accumulating, classifying, and providing essential data upon which such judgments can be based.

To the corporation, a number of definite advantages accrue from a continuing program of meetings with analysts; these advantages extend well beyond merely satisfying legal and regulatory requirements. The constant updating of meaningful information will serve to avoid surprises in the financial community upon the issuance of corporate earnings reports and news releases. Stability in the price of the company's securities will thus be increased and, in time, the investment value of the securities will be enhanced.

The willingness of corporations to meet with analysts on a programmed basis, year after year, through good times and bad, encourages analysts to follow corporate activities, to issue progress reports, and, possibly, to make recommendations for the purchase of the company's securities. Establishing such rapport with analysts and keeping their interest depend upon management's providing assurance that contacts will always be maintained, that interviews will be scheduled whenever required, and that all legitimate questions will be answered without delay.

WHEN AND HOW DO YOU MEET WITH ANALYSTS?

An investor relations program has much in common with that of industrial marketing. The directors of both must identify their prospects, meet with them, establish interest and understanding, present a point of view, and maintain relationships and continuity after the first meeting.

If a company is a leader in its industry or locality, if it has launched a range of new products or developed new processes, or if investment interest has zeroed in on its industry, a certain number of analysts will contact the company on an unsolicited basis. Analysts will also contact individual companies for discussions and reviews when they are preparing studies of their industry.

In making unsolicited calls, analysts often require specific information on a spot basis to complete their reports, or they may have deadlines for a meeting, publication, or presentation. Sometimes analysts may merely be on a fishing expedition for new investment ideas. No matter what prompted the call, a company has much to gain by setting up a meeting with the analyst at the earliest possible time, preferably in the company's offices, where background data and corporate reports are on hand and company executives may be available for interview if the investor relations executive feels it would be of value.

Unsolicited calls are but one facet of the company's relationships with security analysts and, if relied upon excessively, will leave an investor relations program to the whims of chance. In order to achieve fullest benefits from an investor relations program, companies should initiate contacts with analysts on a planned and programmed basis.

The starting point in meeting with analysts should be the same for all companies. Initially, meetings are arranged with analysts on the basis of current shareholder listings for brokers and institutions as shown in shareholder lists and transfer sheets. Brokerage houses with major holdings of customer stock in Street name, mutual funds, banks, insurance companies, pension funds, and other organizations are indicated in these documents.

The advantage of contacting analysts who represent current shareholders is that these analysts have an immediate interest in the company, generally have some background and familiarity with its activities, and will usually be receptive to scheduling a meeting. By providing these shareholders with continuity of information, companies encourage them to maintain their investment and, perhaps, increase their holdings.

After meeting with analysts representing current shareholders, the next point of contact would logically be to meet with other broker analysts. A truly effective investor relations program will first determine the investment characteristics of a company's securities and then work toward establishing and maintaining analyst contacts within the context of these characteristics.

Many factors influence an analyst's interest in meeting with a company, including sales and earnings, the industries in which it operates, and its assets, capitalization, and amount of securities in public hands. Obviously, major well-known companies with significant holdings of their stock in public hands will be important to national brokerage houses. Regional brokers will often want to maintain contact with these companies in order to provide research services competitive with national firms. Even local brokers, doing business where the company is headquartered, may attempt to establish close relationships in order to become investment authorities on corporations within their geographic area.

Smaller, lesser-known companies will often encounter difficulties in telling their story to brokerage house analysts, and the reason is strictly one of economics. Brokers' earnings are generated by commission business, which in turn is developed through a sales staff that must present salable, sound investment concepts and specific advice to institutional or individual investors. Brokers, even the largest ones, can afford to follow only a limited number of companies, and many of them attempt to specialize in order to establish reputations as experts and authorities in particular geographic areas, industries, investment concepts, special situations, or technical analysis.

The amount of stock in public hands must also be taken into account, and enough stock must be available for trading to enable a broker to develop significant commission business through recommendations which his analyst makes and which his sales staff presents to the firm's clients. However, small companies with a limited amount of stock in public hands need not despair of developing interest among analysts providing their business is sound and the future looks reasonably bright. Every area of the country has a number of brokers who, because of their limited resources and small sales staff, specialize in and attempt to develop reputations as authorities on such companies.

Line of business also plays a major role in developing a company's relationship with analysts. In the investment climate of the 1970s, investor relations executives representing companies with clearly delineated product lines in a single industry have an advantage in obtaining a hearing in the financial community. This is based on the degree of specialization among analysts and the need for thorough research, which limits the amount of time an analyst can spend with companies doing business in a number of industrial areas and markets.

Conglomerates and companies that are highly diversified require a more intensive, consistent, and thorough investor relations program than the so-called single-industry companies, which operate within clearly defined areas. Their investor relations executives must often provide analysts with more complete background data, industry evaluations, marketing information, and financial reviews than would be required by analysts following single-industry companies. The certainty that information will be continuous and consistent and that surprises will be avoided tends to encourage interest in multimarket companies.

ORGANIZING MEETINGS WITH ANALYSTS

It is essential to clearly establish the role to be played by each corporate executive who participates in meetings with the analyst. Typically, major organizations assign the investor relations function to a staff executive, who both administers the program and acts as spokesman for the company. In other instances the investor relations function is administered and organized by a staff executive (either as a single responsibility or part of his overall function), with the chief executive officer or other senior executive acting as corporate spokesman. Small companies often employ an outside investor relations counsel, who administers the program and arranges meetings at which a corporate executive speaks for the company. It is never appropriate for the outside investor relations counsel to act as company spokesman unless he has the same access to corporate information and the same responsibility and trust within the company as a staff executive would have.

No matter how the program is organized or administered, and regardless of who speaks for the company, certain practices should be followed in relationships with analysts. First, there should be a single contact point for analysts, either an individual executive or a member of his staff, and all correspondence, calls, and inquiries should be directed to that contact. This sounds simple, but not many telephone operators, receptionists, or even line executives know who handles contacts with the financial community.

Second, while publicity releases, financial reports, and speeches can be reviewed in advance by senior executives and legal counsel, discussions with analysts and answers to their questions involve spot decisions. Therefore, the spokesman for the company should have full access to corporation information, reports, and plans and be thoroughly conversant with the workings of the financial community and the functions and responsibilities of financial analysts. It is essential, too, that he be aware of his own legal responsibility and that of others who speak for the company. The company spokesman must also see to it that corporate ground rules are established and adhered to in discussions with analysts.

CATEGORIES OF MEETINGS

Arranging meetings with analysts involves a wide number of options, which range from meeting with a single analyst to organizing a major meeting at which dozens of analysts will participate. Possibilities may also include appearances before analyst societies.

Ideally, and providing the investor relations executive has the authority, knowledge, and background to be the spokesman for his company, many of the meetings will be scheduled on an individual basis. However, if the chief executive officer is the spokesman for the company, individual meetings will have to be severely limited to avoid excessive drain on his time.

Individual meetings with analysts can be scheduled as the salesman arranges his sales calls. Typically, an hour is a comfortable amount of time. On the other hand, if the analyst is preparing a report or needs to develop background data, he may require considerably more time and perhaps a number of meetings.

Meetings should be designed first to establish rapport between the analyst and the company and then to consider in depth markets, processes, financial matters, accounting procedures, and any other aspects of the company beyond what is covered in the annual report, Form 10-K, publicity releases, fact books, and other documents. The analyst is expected to have familiarized himself with the essential corporation reports and data prior to the meeting. While making an appointment, the investor relations executive may appropriately ask whether the analyst's file on the company is complete and then offer to send missing documents for review in advance of the meeting.

In preparing for meetings, the company spokesman will find it advantageous to develop a rather complete, portable set of files for continuing reference outside his office. But no matter how complete his data may be, questions will invariably arise that cannot be answered on the spot. This is normal and to be expected. A follow-up call or letter can provide appropriate answers and will also present an opportunity for further review and elaboration of critical matters.

There is no harm in arranging a meeting that will include several analysts as long as they are reasonably compatible and have similar objectives in meeting with the company. Analysts often like to review their findings with others in their profession who cover the same corporate areas, and joint meetings can provide such an opportunity. Discussions are often more stimulating when several points of view are presented. On the other hand, it would not be appropriate to include others in a meeting for which one analyst is preparing a report on the company and requires considerable individual assistance.

Organizing meetings with an even larger number of analysts, perhaps a dozen or so, either in financial centers or at corporate headquarters, has a definite place in the investor relations program. However, such meetings differ from those involving a single analyst, or a few analysts, and change their structure from an informal give-and-take discussion into a more formal presentation. At such meetings, analysts would expect to talk with the chief executive officer of the company or other senior management executives. Staff and line executives can be included in the presentation if their areas of operation are of particular interest to the analysts. It is important, though, that those who speak with analysts make a reasonably good appearance and be thoroughly and specifically briefed in advance on the matters to be covered at the meeting.

Chief executive officers differ greatly in their ability to communicate with financial analysts, in their interest in meeting with representatives of the financial community, and in their willingness to engage in meaningful dialog.

Nevertheless, analysts who report on a company or are making investment recommendations should be able to meet with the chief executive and hear firsthand about his philosophy, plans, concepts, and approach. Factual data covering all corporate activities should be reviewed in advance by the company spokesman. If necessary, specific briefings can also be held by the staff or line executives prior to the analyst's meeting with the chief executive officer. Corporate meetings with analysts, especially those that include senior corporate executives, involve two-way communications in which analysts obtain information about the company and, in turn, discuss activities of the financial community that may be of interest to the company officials.

Appearing at meetings of analyst societies has a definite place in the investor relations program. It may be particularly meaningful for a company to meet with societies located in the same city as its corporate headquarters, in areas in which the company has key facilities or major shareholders, or where there is significant interest in its activities. Invitations are sometimes extended to the company by a society's program chairman, or by a broker who is actively recommending the company's securities or, perhaps, working with the company in various financial areas. Also, the company itself can approach the program chairman and offer to appear at a meeting. It may happen that a corporation scheduled to address a society finds it advisable to cancel or postpone its appearance. The investor relations executive who is in a position to arrange meetings on short notice may wish to place his company on a standby basis in order to schedule a meeting in advance of the normal waiting period.

Meeting with the New York Society of Security Analysts provides unique advantages and also poses special problems. First there are ground rules as to minimum corporate size, number of shareholdings, and size of trading volume, and then there are regulations as to the presentation itself. The New York forum provides a company with an attendance of perhaps forty to over two hundred analysts who have varying degrees of interest in the company and its presentation. Press coverage can be more extensive than at other meetings, and reprints of the remarks carry a certain weight with shareholders and the public. Companies in specialized industries, which are of interest to a limited number of analysts, often prefer to appear before so-called splinter groups of analysts representing these industries. Nevertheless, for broad coverage of major corporations, for review of developments currently making headlines, and for exposure of newly listed companies, the New York Society meetings provide excellent forums.

MEETINGS WITH INSTITUTIONAL INVESTORS

Whenever a corporate executive talks with an analyst who represents a broker–dealer, he is indirectly talking to the hundreds, or hundreds of thousands, of individuals and institutions who do business with that broker. There is no other way for a corporation to communicate with individuals who are not its shareholders, except through a financial advertising campaign, which is no substitute for personal relationships with analysts in developing and maintaining a broad interest in the corporation and its securities.

Traditionally, institutional investors, such as bank trust departments, insurance companies, and pension funds, establish investment programs and purchase securities on the advice and recommendation of the brokers' salesmen. These salesmen in turn are guided by their analysts through research reports and by continued monitoring of the securities markets and of prospects for individual companies. The cost of research services is for the most part included in commissions paid to brokers for the purchase or sale of securities.

Despite their continued reliance on brokers for investment research, many institutions are strengthening their own research departments, adding analysts and, at times, making independent evaluations of corporate securities. Through memberships in analyst societies, institutional analysts attend corporate presentations and establish direct contact with corporate executives.

Thus the investor relations executives will, in the normal course of events, meet with institutional analysts and receive unsolicited requests for individual meetings. However, just as with broker analysts, considerable advantage will accrue to a company through a planned, consistent, and continuing program for meeting and maintaining relationships with analysts representing institutional investors.

The first step in scheduling meetings with institutional analysts is to review the company's shareholder list and contact analysts representing institutional shareholders. Most will be pleased with the opportunity to establish direct lines of communication with the company and will generally request that additional meetings be scheduled on a regular basis.

Frequently, meetings with institutional analysts are arranged by brokers who have issued reports on the company's securities or are acting as investment bankers to the company. The broker will usually invite from ten to fifty analysts to a luncheon, at which the company's chief executive or other management executives discuss corporate activities. Usually three-way benefits are derived from these meetings. The broker generates commission business for his salesmen; the company is provided with a preselected group of potential shareholders whose investment decisions will be affected by the presentation; and the institutional analyst can form judgments and make recommendations with the advantage of having had personal contact with corporate executives.

When meetings are arranged by brokers or analyst societies, the company may play a role in selecting the audience, but this option is often limited. Therefore, the company may wish from time to time to arrange its own meetings with institutional analysts. Such meetings provide unique opportunities for engaging in dialog with potential investors. Individual meetings with institutional analysts are valuable follow-ups to these group meetings and enable the investor relations executive to solidify relationships with those institutions his company would prefer as shareholders.

What Does the Analyst Want to Know?

Investors often take a simplistic view of the analyst's capabilities. They tend to define good analysts as those who recommend stocks that move up after buy recommendations are issued and down after sell recommendations. This way of looking at the analyst's function and judging his capabilities may have a degree of validity, but it fails to take into account the time span involved or extraneous factors that are beyond the scope of his accountability.

Day-by-day fluctuations in the price of corporate securities and longer term trends can be influenced by factors other than fundamental corporate developments. A few of these are national politics and international relationships, interest rate levels, changes in the economic outlook, inflation expectations, ecological considerations, and labor negotiations in major industries. Stock prices are also influenced by technical considerations such as selling versus buying pressures; speculative interest in certain industries or companies; tax considerations; recommendations of brokerage houses; and trends in institutional investing.

Obviously, then, analysts need be concerned with many more factors than the basic position of a company. A sound background in economics is a valuable asset, as are an understanding of financial matters, appreciation of political factors that may affect the stock market, insight into the cyclical nature of consumer or industrial demand, and knowledge about the life cycle of products. In addition, analysts should become involved in those technical stock market factors which affect stock prices and in such related matters as stockholder mix, trends in stock trading, and insider transactions.

Essentially, the analyst, in his meetings with corporate management and in his evaluation of company prospects, is attempting to arrive at answers to two separate sets of questions. The first involves expectations for the company in terms of sales, profits, and a range of other operating and financial results. The second is concerned with a judgment as to how securities markets will evaluate these factors. This evaluation is referred to as the company's price–earnings multiple, which is the price of its stock divided by current or expected earnings. It's the number of times at which the market is willing to pay for earnings.

The most critical factor in security analysis involves an evaluation of management. As a guide to the future, the analyst reviews past decisions in such areas as expansion, financing, research, and marketing. He also studies past corporate reports, releases, speeches, and other documents to compare past expectations with actual realization. He has discussions with the chief executive and other senior executives in order to gain an insight into their philosophy and concepts. Often, talking with customers and suppliers can give him valuable information on how corporate managers run their business and exercise control. As a further source of background in their evaluation management, analysts have become increasingly interested in the qualifications of members of the board of directors—their responsibilities, degree of independence, and shareholdings.

In looking toward future prospects, the analyst may begin with a study of the company's markets and marketing programs. He will scrutinize sales trends, the state of the industry, the maturity of products, new product concepts, price trends, the relative importance of the economic cycle, the strengths and weaknesses of the sales force, and a range of economic considerations.

The analyst will also be concerned with the company's production facilities, need for expansion or phasing out of obsolete equipment, pollution problems, depreciation of equipment, and replacement costs. He will need to know about labor relations, unionization, efficiency rates, and competitive factors.

An indication of a company's thrust and direction will be provided by an analysis of research and development programs, of its plans for internal growth and the expansion of product lines. In view of the considerable role acquisitions played in the growth of many corporations in the 1960s, the analyst will be interested in management's views on the desirability of making acquisitions in coming years. He will also attempt to determine whether the company has the financial strength and management capability to make meaningful acquisitions and run them effectively.

As a result of severe financial difficulties experienced by many companies toward the end of the 1960s, analysts have been very much concerned about the basic financial position of those they are studying. In reviewing corporate annual reports, they are paying close attention to comments in the auditor's letter, notes to the financial statements, balance-sheet items, debt position, various financial ratios, and the return on capital, assets, and sales. Through their reviews, analysts will be particularly alert to accounting principles involved and to the way in which various items are reported.

Analysts generally maintain up-to-date files on corporate financial reports and are expected to review these documents prior to meeting with company officials. However, the knowledgeable analyst no longer accepts corporate financial reports, earnings estimates, or forecasts at face value. He will attempt to determine the extent to which costs are capitalized versus expenses for such items as research, engineering, and interest. He will review the character of investments, determine the validity of long-term accounts receivable, and check on the accounting for installment sales, depreciation, taxes, investment credits, and the earnings of subsidiaries.

Corporate financial reporting is becoming increasingly detailed as a result of both the liberalization of disclosure policy on the part of many companies and more stringent reporting requirements on the part of the SEC. Nevertheless, company spokesmen are generally asked by analysts to provide details that are not included in financial reports, on such matters as income taxes, sundry accounts, valuation of inventories, availability of funds for expansion, need for additional working capital, and disposal of unproductive assets.

It is essential that a clearly defined company policy be established covering the way in which financial matters are to be discussed and the extent to which details may be revealed. Above all, advance determination must be made, with appropriate legal guidance, as to what information is to be considered material and consequently not to be revealed on a selective basis.

Through the establishment of proper guidelines, corporate executives should be able, when talking with an individual analyst, to avoid disclosing material information that could be expected to affect the desire of investors to buy, sell, or hold securities. However, it is always possible that such information may be discussed inadvertently or revealed by a corporate executive who has not had adequate briefing on such matters.

Should this occur, remedial action must immediately be taken. The first step is to inform the analyst candidly of what has happened and discuss the implications with him. In this connection, the SEC has established the principle that an analyst becomes an insider when he receives material information on an exclusive basis, and he may not personally benefit from such information or make disclosure to others. Arrangements should then be made by the company for public disclosure of the information through a publicity release, a news conference, or a meeting to which the press is invited.

Investor Relations and Stock Prices

The investor relations executive should not attempt to evaluate publicly the investment merits of his company's stock or to advise investors as to the proper price for the stock. These are functions of the analyst, who, on an unbiased basis, is expected to take into account both stock market and corporate factors, which range from the company's business activities to the entire spectrum of industrial, political, and economic events that can make an impact on the fortunes of an individual company.

The investor relations executive, on the other hand, is expected to be an authority on his company. He represents his company and its chief executive in the financial community and provides corporate, industrial, and financial information to analysts. He is also responsible for presenting his company's philosophy and concepts and for expressing his management's point of view.

Printed
Financial Communications

Richard A. Lewis

OF ALL the literature a corporation produces, the most important by far is the annual report to stockholders. It is a record of the company's performance over the past year and a tangible identification of the firm. But, more importantly, it is the president's basic and most effective selling tool for his company. As such, it reflects his personal taste in design, illustration, and writing.

The chief executive officer who has properly delegated authority doesn't have many specific responsibilities himself, but he must perform his primary function—acting as chief spokesman for the company. Much of his time is spent talking to members of the financial community. He appears before security analyst meetings, has private conversations with important analysts, and talks with investment bankers prior to the sale of securities.

Richard A. Lewis is President, Corporate Annual Reports, Inc., New York, N.Y.

If the annual report does an effective job of giving the company's basic message and answering key questions, the president won't have to repeat it in person. When the people he meets with have been briefed by a thorough annual report, the president can get to a more meaningful level of conversation quickly.

The professional investment community is not the only group reached by the annual report, and the key to understanding this document is to remember that it must be designed and written to say many things to many different audiences.

To the small stockholder, it is primarily a form of assurance. Statistics show that this investor spends only five to ten minutes per annual report, looking for dividend news and checking whether sales and earnings are higher than last year's. He may also glance through the president's letter, primarily for reinforcement of the already positive attitudes toward the company that led him to buy its stock in the first place. Although an annual report by itself isn't likely to persuade a small investor to buy stock, a convincing document may encourage him to hold on to what he owns.

Many of an annual report's readers study it much more closely than does the small stockholder to whom it is ostensibly addressed. To the professional investor or the security analyst, it is the first step in any serious research about a company. It is this man's basic up-to-date source book, the document he reads on the plane as he prepares to visit the company president or investor relations spokesman. The security analyst will often make marginal notes in an annual report, using it as a notebook on the corporation. In addition to basic facts, he is trying to get a sense of the thrust of a company—where it is going, how it will get there, what its strengths are. Until he has visited the executives in person, the annual report is the embodiment of a company.

Another important audience can be found within the brokerage houses: the registered representatives who actually sell to clients, particularly those who specialize in institutions. These people make new research recommendations to their clients, and the annual report is basic to their presentation. Moreover, they are not above complaining about an annual report to a company that doesn't present itself well.

An increasingly significant group is the growing numbers of employees who are stockholders in their own companies. Employee stock purchase plans tie them into the corporation's profit results and identify their self-interest in the company in a more direct way. Some companies also make a regular practice of sending annual reports to employees who are not stockholders. There is a great deal of information about a company that employees are not aware of, and annual reports can give them a perspective about both the company and the people who run it that they probably could not get from their corner of the research lab or assembly line.

Acquisition candidates are another important audience for the annual report; it is usually one of the first items that changes hands and certainly one of the most thoroughly studied by the executives of the company that may be acquired.

The annual report serves in fact as a corporate calling card, a way to impress people the executives are meeting with, particularly foreign businessmen. Because this group —new customers, new suppliers, college students, bankers

—is so large, companies regularly print two to three times as many annual reports as they have stockholders.

The importance of these additional audiences explains why companies spend considerable money on the design and printing of annual reports. Studies indicate an average expenditure of from $.75 to $1.25 per copy. For very short runs (under 10,000) the cost may be higher, and for very long runs (over 100,000), it may be lower.

No less an investment is the time spent by top executives preparing the annual report. In fact, the same executives who are directly involved in producing the report become its most careful cadre of readers. By the time they've read the entire document several times they're bored with it, but they are also more concerned with it and influenced by it than anyone else. For them and the rest of the top executive group, the annual report is a real source of soul-searching analysis, the pointer for the future direction of the company and their own prospects within it.

The annual report attained this eminence and multipurpose role through an evolutionary process that began with the establishment of the Securities and Exchange Commission in 1934. The SEC required only the bare financial facts then, and companies supplied little else in the sparse documents of those early years. Then in 1941, *Financial World* magazine began giving its still-prestigious awards for the best annual reports, adding an element of competition and rewarding companies that provided year-to-year comparisons, financial highlights, and other improvements.

Annual reports changed rapidly and in a different direction in the early 1960s as something new entered the business scene. The major influence was Litton Industries with its bevy of followers, many of them LIDOs ("Litton Industries Drop Outs"), whose executives had caught on to the growth-company game. The game was played by pushing up stock prices and price–earnings ratios through rapid acquisitions—often insignificant companies in mundane industries totally unrelated to the buyer's primary business. The goal was to wrap the whole package of activities with a growth-company image, and the image was built around a dazzling annual report that talked concepts and futures. Although the graphic beauty of the annual report reached a high, the informational quality dropped off as the conglomerates sought to keep people's hopes and dreams alive.

Reality hit with the economic downturn of 1968–1970. Out of the wreckage of this period, and prodded by accountants and the government, a new and much more factually oriented annual report emerged. Where the companies had previously put mystique-oriented photographs that presented an abstract image, they now came back with charts and graphs presenting solid financial facts. The pendulum was swinging the other way.

The trend toward sobriety was further reinforced by new requirements from professional and governmental sources. Both the SEC and the Accounting Principles Board of the American Institute of Certified Public Accountants started pushing for greater disclosure. Under Chairman William J. Casey, sworn in on April 14, 1971, the SEC was revitalized and initiated many improvements. It stressed larger footnotes, in ten-point type, which made them much more readable. The agency also called for a more detailed 10-K annual report to the government, including product-line breakouts. Corporations were pressured to provide the same beakdown information in the annual report to stockholders.

But along with the strictly factual approach, most management teams still want the annual report, above all else, to present the corporation as growth-oriented. In fact, emphasizing the company's basic strengths that will enable it to achieve future growth should be one of its primary goals.

The executive faced with the responsibility of putting out today's annual report has a difficult challenge. On the one hand, the document must not deal in abstract and abstruse concepts; it must be quick and easy to read; it must understate. But on the other hand, the annual report must somehow "turn on" the reader. It must set forth the strengths, assets, and virtues of the company so forcefully —or present its management so convincingly or show its products so intriguingly—that the reader is motivated to learn more about the company and, hopefully, to invest in it. And it must compete against thousands of other annual reports for the attention of investors and analysts. In a particular industry group, the competition is especially keen. When a security analyst begins his industry research and compares the annual reports of direct competitors in the airlines industry, for example, Eastern's annual report would thus compete head-on with those of American, United, and Pan Am.

The annual reports that stand out, year after year, are those that simplify the often complicated corporate picture and present facts in the most direct way possible.

If the executive in charge of putting out the report had a single-word maxim on his desk, that word should be "clarity." The need for it is legal, practical, economic, competitive. Businessmen traditionally have had a tendency to obscure facts, perhaps dating from an era when secretiveness was the rule and disclosure of financial figures wasn't required. Nothing could be more self-defeating to the modern corporation. Clarity and disclosure should be the main considerations in preparing the annual report. The company whose report rambles will confuse and finally lose the attention of the very security analyst upon whose readership the company relies to keep its stock price and price–earnings multiple high. He is the most important target for the report.

One way to achieve clarity and gain favorable attention amid all the competition is to present information in layers, so to speak. The goal is to present the same meaningful information about the corporation to the several different levels of readership, from that of the most casual skimmer to the serious student. The small shareholder may be attracted by the cover, pictures, and captions. A slightly more sophisticated reader might read the president's letter and financial highlights, whereas the most financially sophisticated would want fairly detailed information about operations and financial developments, as well as the footnotes. The technique that enables one annual report to communicate with so many different audiences is the ability to make the different levels of information all impart the same key points. There is a growing trend for less text, for fewer words that say more and are organized to spell out the central message more succinctly and without repetition.

Writing the annual report is often a problem for senior executives; they know so much that they lack the perspective to extract and distill the corporation's primary message amid all the details that tend to distract the reader. Usually the writing chore is best performed by a corporate communications executive, or even a freelance writer. Such a writer can help fight a tendency that grew up in the late 1960s to group business categories under fad labels. A company that makes sewer pipes might label them "environmental equipment"—a bit of sleight of hand that tends to obscure a company and to irritate, confuse, and finally discourage analysts.

Worse than using such labels is actually regrouping manufacturing sections within the company to make its products sound more glamorous. Typically, a company will break down its operations into four or five categories to satisfy the SEC product-line breakout requirement. But some companies are purposefully devious, taking perhaps 20 percent of the business from one division and 30 percent from another and regrouping them under a label like "transportation." Part of the trend toward greater disclosure, compactness, and clarity is to provide product-line breakouts that are related to the company's operating divisions. This is the way the corporation itself keeps records and the way the outside analyst can best understand the company. Even a firm that wants to publicize its growing position in, say, the health care market, should provide elsewhere an accurate and succinct product-line breakout so the analyst can know the different components of an umbrella term that may be used.

Producing an annual report that will meet these many criteria takes resourcefulness and a wide variety of skills. From a publishing standpoint alone, all the factors needed to put out any book or magazine are there—the design, writing, and organizational talent, the production scheduling, and quality control procedures. But complicating the job enormously are the many executives in the corporation who have responsibility for, or want a voice in, producing the annual report. The executive in charge of the report has to cope with the ambitious vice president, the financial department, the house counsel, and the outside accountants. Somehow he has to either win their confidence or reconcile their differing viewpoints. Sometimes even the president and the chairman aren't in agreement. And finally, after the document is practically finished, a whole new group of people may be invited into the picture, including perhaps the president's wife or his secretary. Everyone has an opinion about the cover photo, the wording of a caption, the size of the headlines.

Since there are so many different ways to handle a subjective work like this, the only viable solution is the one companies are increasingly using—putting the annual report project into stronger hands, possibly a vice president of corporate communications or vice president of investor relations, someone closer to the president who automatically has more authority and can make firmer decisions. This person must be an expert on every aspect of the job, and it must be so thoroughly thought out that he is ready to explain exactly why the photo of a certain product is right for the cover, and to explain it with the weight of authority. Even so, it is often helpful to hire an outside consultant whose experience can add further clout to the opinions of the corporate executive in charge of the annual report.

Perhaps the most important strategy for launching the annual report project is to write a plan that sets forth specific objectives. The plan might involve establishing a theme to be followed—presenting the company's young management team, featuring its strong position as a multinational company, showing the new plants that promise greater productivity, presenting the company's research capability. In addition to giving the book a unified look and a more focused point of view that helps security analysts and other readers remember the company's message, the theme enables the annual report team to defend its decisions against the many other recommendations about pictures to be used and subjects to be included. For example, if the pictorial theme is new facilities, there is an immediate and clear-cut reason why a new-product photo can't be included.

After a plan has been written that includes a statement of objectives and the means to implement them, it should then go to the president for approval. After that, it can be circulated among other key executives, who shouldn't usually have much to add after the president has endorsed it.

The plan should also include a schedule, which must be revised if any of the key target dates are missed. The schedule is an important aid to the annual report executive in many ways: If he respects the deadlines and maintains his own commitments, he will find that fellow executives are likely to contribute their segments with comparable precision and orderliness. If he doesn't take the deadlines seriously, the whole book will slide into a crisis situation at the very end, which will be costly and wasteful and ultimately result in an unsuccessful document.

The schedule depends upon the company's fiscal year, and the pivotal point is the date on which the accountants can provide the financial statements. For a company using the calendar year, the figures should be available in late January or early February. Working backward, the plan should be presented to the president in September, and the photography and writing should be developed from late September through November. During the same period, a design for the book should be worked out, and most of the copy should be written in final form to fit the space and incorporated into a dummy book, which the president can read over the Christmas holidays. If the president is decisive and stands by the plan he approved earlier, any differences between him and other key executives could be reconciled during January, and the book can be finished from a production standpoint as soon as the figures come in from the accountants. Their deadline must be clear in advance; in a recent survey conducted by my firm, getting these audited figures was named the third biggest problem in putting out the annual report. (Reconciling the different viewpoints of senior management members came first, and getting good photography on time was second.)

Based on the accountants' deadline to provide figures, the printer must be scheduled. Bids should be solicited well before Christmas so that a final selection can be made and a printer contacted in plenty of time. The usual number of working days required to print an annual report—don't count Saturday and Sunday—is from nine to fifteen, and the specific days must be reserved for your project. Color photos must be released five or six weeks before press date.

The corporate executive in charge of the annual report can't possibly become an expert on every production detail; this is why so many companies hire an outside public relations agency or a graphic design firm to act as a subcontractor. To keep the lines of responsibility clear, the man in the company should deal from then on only with his key subcontractor, who in turn coordinates the whole job. The graphic design firm can be expected to provide an initial design that meets the company's stated objectives, hire the photographer and negotiate with him, and guarantee on-time photographs that meet all the requirements. The design firm should also handle all typesetting, work with the in-company executive on fitting the writing and design together to create a dummy book, prepare the finished mechanical boards that are provided to the printer, and supervise the entire printing process.

If properly used, the graphic design firm helps the corporation keep within its printing budget. Careful advance planning and scheduling, and early decisions on any corrections or changes, are the only ways to avoid costly waste. There are three major stages where costs for changes mount unnecessarily: when the book is being typeset, when the mechanicals are being pasted down, and after the whole thing goes to the printer. Changes cost more at each succeeding stage. Retouching a photo to eliminate the chairman's jowls might cost $50 when the photo is first received; the same change could cost $650 after the engravings have been made and as much as $2,000 in the blueprint stage just before printing, when it requires repeating several different steps at overtime rates.

If not kept under control, unnecessary changes in type —called author's alterations, or AAs—can double the basic typesetting charge. A normal cost is some $2,500 to $3,000 for setting enough type for a thirty-two-page annual report, including financials. Changes may easily run from $1,000 to $2,500 and have been known to reach $10,000 to $15,-000. Even more inexcusable are printing changes after the book goes to the printer. A full day is allowed for legitimate corrections, but should changes make a book miss its press deadline, costs soar. The many steps required to make corrected plates are all paid for at premium rates; a four-color press may wait at a regular $200 an hour or $300 on a weekend; all overtime labor is paid at time and a half; and an additional weekend premium can run from $700 to $1,500 a day.

Many of these problems can be prevented if the executive in charge of the annual report makes sure the other executives involved "sign off" the project at key stages— preferably on the first proofs. He alone should work with the designer after the main sign-off date by the president or chairman.

An often neglected area, but one that is important from

both cost and deadline points of view, is mailing. Its considerations must be built into every stage of the annual report schedule. According to the *Corporate Communications Report* newsletter, time should be allowed for a sample of the annual report dummy to be tested on the mailer's equipment, for his envelopes to be tested in the mail for durability, and for printed company information to be carefully checked. Mailing the report third class bulk will greatly reduce postage, but five weeks are required for delivery.

The annual report that is a good ambassador for its company should be distributed as widely as possible among potential stockholders and the investment community. To reach them, a good medium at reasonable prices is provided by the cooperative annual report advertising sections published each year by such publications as *Financial World,* the *National Observer, Forbes,* and *The New York Times.* Usually just the cover is shown, with a small block of copy about the company and an offer to send the report to respondents. My firm surveyed the more than 350 companies that used these media in 1972, and found that most of them used the ads to broaden investor interest among individuals (83 percent) and among the financial community (74 percent). They were generally pleased with the results: 41 percent felt the ads helped increase the number of shareholders, and 83 percent felt they helped make the company better known. Costs ranged from $265 at *Financial World,* where requests for annual reports averaged 800, to $995 for two appearances in *The New York Times,* with an average of 3,000 to 4,000 responses. Of course, printing costs for the extra copies of the report and mailing and handling costs must be added, but once a company has taken the trouble to produce an effective annual report, it makes good business sense to advertise and distribute it to the maximum audience.

Other printed communications issued by a corporation include quarterly reports, postmeeting reports, press releases, advertising, magazines, newsletters, anniversary books, and factbooks.

Interim reports represent one of the greatest potentials for upgrading the overall level of corporate communications. General Electric has introduced an interesting innovation—quarterly "magazines." All but the annual report issue carry up to four pages of advertising bought by various GE divisions, which helps pay for production of the magazines, encourages stockholder involvement, and measures response. An offer for a $12 set of rechargeable batteries got 15,000 returns from the 700,000 shareholders. The company's medical products division bought a full page ad to reach shareholders who might sit on hospital boards and be influential in purchases. Editorially, these magazines stress a section called "What Investors Are Asking" to inform the shareholders what questions professional investors have been raising about the company.

In the present business climate of fast change and pressure for disclosure—possibly with profit projections coming up—it is imperative that companies do a better job of reporting on a quarterly basis, whatever format they decide to use. Many firms overlook obvious ways to do this. For example, the SEC now requires 10-Q quarterly reports, which include balance-sheet information, but very few companies put this information in their quarterly reports to shareholders. Another way to upgrade interim reports is to issue them in an 8½″ x 11″ newsletter format. Companies invite being ignored when they issue small statements on flimsy paper that fit into a small envelope and tend to get lost in the bottom of a file drawer. One analyst we know files the press releases sent by the companies he follows but not their quarterly reports—since they get lost.

Postmeeting reports have gone in an opposite direction, away from the rather elaborate books that came out in the mid-1960s. The annual meeting has been somewhat de-emphasized; in fact, many companies now incorporate their annual meeting report into the first-quarter interim report. But no matter how these publications are handled, it is certainly appropriate to report on the annual meeting, whether in a separate booklet or in the quarterly report. And the information should be distributed as quickly as possible after the meeting. The postmeeting report, like any financial information, loses all value in today's fast-changing market if it is delayed even a week beyond the minimum time required to publish it.

Wall Street is becoming more and more conscious of the high cost of original research, and the growing need for easily accessible, solid facts about a company is giving rise to an important new kind of financial communication— the corporate factbook. Written specifically for the professional investor, the factbook gives a highly detailed presentation about the company, its management, its philosophy, its financial position, and its markets. In addition, it should include the latest industry statistics and other types of general information—material that is time-consuming to gather, but essential for a good research report.

The factbook is of prime importance to multi-industry companies, which increasingly face the frustration of simply being ignored by analysts because they are too complicated to follow.

As we project the trend, these new factbooks will be

unpretentious, probably with typewritten copy instead of printed copy, and will be intended for a small audience of perhaps some two hundred interested security analysts. Of course, in observance of legal and ethical requirements for disclosure, the factbook would be available to all shareholders along with all the other corporate literature, but in practice, few would want to bother with such detailed information.

Both factbooks and more detailed, informative annual reports are an outgrowth of the fact that the research dollar is shrinking in Wall Street. It is shrinking because negotiated commissions do not allow as much commission money as before to finance the salaries of security analysts. As a result, the burden of providing much of the detailed financial information about a company is shifting from the analysts to the company itself. If the trend continues it will add a large new responsibility to the investor relations function.

No longer will it be enough merely to respond to analyst questions and provide annual and quarterly reports. It will be necessary instead to develop and present a complete data base from which the investment decision process can begin. The analyst would then have the much less time-consuming job of assessing the quality of the company-prepared information, delving into areas he thinks need more research, talking to management, and reaching his conclusions.

Investor Relations
in Europe

William F. Brackman

THE RISING EMINENCE of the foreign capital market in U.S. investor relations planning is neither surprising nor accidental. Already accounting for some 20 percent of all trading in American securities, foreign capital markets are robust, growing much faster than our own, and make up an additional source for potential investors.

Europe in particular has led the way in investing as foreign purchases of U.S. securities increased from $3.7 billion in 1960 to about $30 billion in 1972. So, the reasons for beginning an overseas investor relations program, if you don't already have one, continue to multiply.

Each company has its own reasons for going to international capital markets—whether to build a broader following for current listings, to develop new sources for debt financing, to secure local currencies for overseas expansion,

William F. Brackman is Vice President, Investor Relations, The Gillette Company, Boston, Mass.

or to create less costly alternate sources of financing during tight-credit periods such as we experienced in the United States during 1970 and 1971. My own company began its program some time ago as a result of some $100 million in Eurodollar debentures, which are convertible into Gillette common. Our hope is that when the conversions occur, Europeans will continue to hold Gillette stock.

CONSIDER THE DIFFERENCES

Although the need for sound investments is as real to Europeans as it is to anyone else, there are a few basic differences to consider before laying out any program. These involve the type of investor, the nature of your contacts, and the basis for establishing and maintaining a relationship.

First, the small investor in Europe is by no means the market force he is in this country. Foreign trading is done almost exclusively by institutions—principally the large commercial and private banks—dealing for themselves or for the accounts of wealthy depositors, major trusts, pensions and companies, and even government entities investing surplus funds. Although New York Stock Exchange member firms have been moving into Europe, their branches have not developed the man-in-the-street concept to the magnitude we see among American investors; nor have they displaced the traditional traders, the banks.

Europeans, like all of us, are looking for traditional investment safeguards that American equities can provide: liquid investment, safety of capital, growth potential, stability, and, to a greater extent than we are accustomed to in America, protection against currency fluctuations. European investments tend more to be long term as well. Europeans therefore welcome the openness of American corporations in reporting their operations, finances, earnings, and other particulars—information that their domestic corporations are not required to provide.

Investor contacts should be handled only by a corporate officer, usually the person charged with financial relations in the United States. His relationships with European bankers will be somewhat different, however, from his domestic analyst activities. To begin with, you do not wait for them to call you when they're interested in learning more about your company; and we, at least, do not meet them en masse as we do before American analyst societies. Instead, we call them and ask for a private appointment to tell them why we think our company merits their investment consideration. The mountain, in effect, goes to Muhammad.

Just one trip or visit, or an irregular or inconsistent program, will do more harm than good. The European investor is for the most part a long-term investor and he looks for a long-term relationship, which is years in the building.

Establish Your Contacts

Before you go to Europe, you have to know who the important bankers are and arrange to meet their best people. The logical source of this information is your own investment banker; he is familiar with the major trading establishments, has many contacts inside these banks, and will be glad to help set up your initial appointments. A single major investment banker is sufficient for some firms, but other companies are more comfortable using a different banking contact in each country, principally to avoid being identified with a single banking establishment. Several major U.S. companies also are working their programs almost exclusively through large local European banks, one advantage being that it gives them stronger identification with the local capital market and emphasizes their commitment to doing business in those countries. They often feel, too, that a local bank has a better insider's view as to who is most important and influential in the capital market.

Whichever you choose, the bank or banks will provide lists of institutions that ought to be on your agenda, usually coordinating them with lists of your known shareholders. Quite often you'll find that public relations or management consultants can complement these lists, but the banker will be your most valuable source of information and contacts.

There are so many different institutions throughout Europe that it is extremely important for you to get advice on potential contacts from your investment banker, assuming he is knowledgeable about Europe, or from an American institutional brokerage firm that is involved in the European market.

The individuals they'll most likely come up with will be investment officers and security analysts in state-owned or private banks, usually senior officers of their establishments. All will have U.S. contacts or relationships or their own branches, and all will be trading principally on the various U.S. exchanges. They subscribe regularly to investment reports put out by American institutional brokerage firms, particularly those cultivating a European clientele, and are reasonably conversant with who's who in the stock market.

Beyond this, some companies, such as Gillette, have been household words in Europe for generations and were known to the fathers of the current bankers. Such companies have large and visible operations and marketing programs within the United Kingdom and Europe, and this is a definite plus in breaking the ice.

Even billion-dollar companies, however, will be surprised to find how little they are known in Europe despite prominent positions on U.S. stock exchanges and impressive financial credentials. Without some visibility in Europe beyond the analyst reports the banks receive, there is little opportunity for any company to stand out in the European investor's consciousness. Thus your banker's assistance becomes all that much more valuable in emphasizing the value of personal contacts.

PLAN YOUR APPROACH

Having identified the major traders, there are several ways to proceed. Our preference has been to make personal calls on the institutions that have been singled out as most important. Other companies prefer to conduct group meetings with twenty to forty bankers, held either totally or partially in the local language and including slide presentations, company films dubbed in the local language, and so forth. You can have it either way or both, but I personally feel the personal visit is the more productive approach.

We've found it practical to begin setting up our appointments some four to six weeks in advance of the visit, starting with a letter of self-introduction that states the purpose of the visit and why the particular institution is being contacted, and affirms that the visit will be part of a long-range investor relations program in Europe. (Your banker should be willing to handle this initial introduction.) I generally suggest we meet in the banker's office rather than at lunch, where opportunity for serious discussion is more limited.

In planning each day of the visit, figure on having your first interview at 9 A.M. and your last one very late in the day by our standards. Because of the time lag, U.S. stock exchanges and banks close very late in Europe, and it is traditional for many bankers to work as late as 8 and 9 P.M. Plan it so that the average interview will run almost exactly one hour (that is about all you'll need if you're well organized), and you'll have the flexibility to schedule efficiently.

After confirming your appointment, send ahead an annual report, annual meeting report, the latest quarterly, and perhaps a 10-K form, so that the banker can brief himself as fully as he likes for your visit. Also bring along additional reference sources, such as recent analyst presentations, reprints of corporate features, or similar materials.

As part of their overseas investor relations program, many companies feel that it is necessary to translate their annual reports, 10-Ks, and other materials into major foreign languages. While this does have some obvious advantages, we do not translate ours, and have not found this to be a barrier or a deterrent to carrying out our program.

If additional quarterly or annual earnings reports are issued prior to your visit, you might consider telexing the results to your public relations counsel or your company's internal PR department overseas for translation and further telexing to the principal financial journals of Europe.

In any event, the timely disclosure of significant information such as earnings, major new products, and the like should figure as strongly in your overseas investor relations plans as it does domestically.

The Interview

Your interview will probably be with one or two of the senior investment officers of the bank. Although Europe has a growing fraternity of security analysts, at present they generally tend to be junior officers with lesser responsibility for making investment decisions, though this is changing as the profession matures.

Do not expect the same reaction you'd get from an American analyst. Because you have sought out the original meeting and crossed the Atlantic to make the appointment, the ball is in your court.

Most important of all, do not expect to be interviewed as you are in the United States. You will be expected to volunteer information and they will listen attentively; questions will come a little later. I have often said as an opening approach that Gillette has a continuing policy to visit European institutions at least once a year so that they may discuss our company on a personal basis with a company officer. This allows me an opportunity to comment on our current operations and any other timely news, such as new products, product progress, organization, management, and perhaps acquisitions, if pertinent. I can also encourage their questions on any matters concerning them that have not been adequately covered in U.S. analyst reports they have received. There are times when incomplete information can cause them to have a somewhat distorted view of your company, and you now have a good opportunity to put matters in proper perspective.

They will be most pleased if you are candid and straightforward in your comments and answers. It is not that they are seeking confidential or inside information, but they would be inclined to lose interest if you constantly hedge in your reply. After all, you have come a long way to discuss your company with them—so discuss it.

Be careful and conscious of your choice of words. Even though they all speak and understand English, it is wise to use simple words, speak fairly slowly and distinctly, and avoid slang expressions. This is not the time to use your full vocabulary of shadings or nuances. You can commit a major error if they misunderstand what you are trying to say.

We've found it a good practice to bring each banker up to date on our current operations, particularly as they relate to his own country. Include comments on new products, successful marketing programs, organizational strengths, management setup, important acquisitions or expansions, and other timely information.

You might use part of your hour or so to find out some important things from him that will help you in future visits as well as in shaping other parts of your European investor relations program. For instance, you may sound him out on successful practices of other American companies he deals with.

Once you've had your meetings, it is extremely difficult to get a precise feeling about how well your story has gone over or how many shareholders have been added as a result. For one thing, Europeans prefer a great deal of anonymity in their stock purchases—their own exchanges, in fact, deal primarily in bearer securities with dividend coupons which are unregistered—and foreign purchases generally are left in a Street name with their

American branch or affiliate. We have also attempted, without success, to obtain tax data from the U.S. Internal Revenue Service that would let us know how much of our dividend payments are made to foreign holders.

There are guidelines, however. One is participation by foreign banks or securities dealers in new issues, and another, certainly, is the amount of preparation your contacts will make prior to your second visit. A great many companies similar to ours now have large bond issues totally in foreign hands, a certain endorsement for the success of our programs.

THE FOLLOW-UP

Beyond the initial visit, what do you do next? For one thing, you've added some important names to your analyst mailing list. I have previously mentioned the advisability of issuing earnings reports and other major announcements simultaneously in foreign financial capitals. I might point out, however, that the European financial press is far less receptive to corporate information from U.S. companies than are our own financial wire services and publications. It is often true that unless your company's securities are listed on the local exchanges or your own operations in the respective market are significant, you will be ignored by the financial press.

The *Financial Times* of London, for instance, is the leading financial journal in the United Kingdom and one of the world's leading publications in its field. Yet it seldom discusses a company's results unless that company is quoted on the London exchange, as Gillette is. Often, however, U.S. correspondents of publications such as the

Financial Times will do corporate articles and discuss general financial results as part of their features. This is an area where international financial public relations counsel can be invaluable in helping to maintain your corporate visibility between annual visits.

The matter of whether or not to list on foreign exchanges is always under consideration by those conducting overseas investor relations programs, and until now the consensus has run against listing on most of these boards. Gillette is listed on a number of foreign exchanges now and may consider additional listings in the future.

For one thing, European stock trading is very fragmented. The London Stock Exchange is by far the largest in the Common Market, with some $22 billion in trades annually. This is four times the volume registered on the Paris Bourse, which is considered the chief contender for dominance of Common Market equity trading. So again we come back to the observation that trading on European exchanges is very light by our standards and that small investors are not very active. Institutions account for less than 13 percent of the trading in Paris, while more than 50 percent of all trades are under $400. The savings rates in Europe are extremely high, however, and capital is moving more freely between countries. Should European companies begin to pay more attention to small investors and go after their savings with a changed attitude, including fuller disclosure, then the picture may change and some additional listings may become advisable. It bears watching.

On the other hand, the purchase of securities from U.S. exchanges is very easy for European traders, and a number of moves are under way to make trading on our exchanges easier and more economical for foreigners and to build greater interest among both Europeans and the Japanese in trading on U.S. exchanges. The New York Stock Exchange and the American Exchange are both actively promoting international trading, and the Midwest Exchange admits foreign members. The Midwest's board has approved in principle a 40 percent discount off public brokerage rates to certain broker–dealers, initially to those from the London Stock Exchange. One advantage of such an arrangement would be the admission of U.S. member firms to overseas exchanges with the possibility of a substantial increase in the level of trading done in those markets.

In any event, foreign interest in our shares will continue to grow for a variety of reasons, and our efforts overseas should be more productive as a result.

What else can an investment relations officer do to make his program more successful? You can build on your annual visits to the bankers by inviting them, their fellow officers, and analysts to visit your corporate headquarters when they're in this country. You can explore similar ways to broaden relationships with their affiliates and associates in the United States. Often investment bankers are asked to assist foreign analysts in putting together a U.S. itinerary; let your banker know you're interested.

Another technique is to build up your relationships wherever possible with American brokerage firms and institutional investors that are aggressively pursuing European business. Many companies have appeared before security analyst and banker groups overseas under the sponsorship of major American brokerage houses active in those financial markets. This may be a productive approach to reach a great many people if you're unable to devote the time and effort to private annual visits.

I've always felt that you don't get as many higher-echelon executives at these meetings as you do in visits to the banks, but others may feel different about it. In any event, this sort of meeting is likely to become a more successful practice as the broadening interest in U.S. investments fuels a corresponding rise in the number, influence, and investment authority of European analysts, and also as the small investor becomes more active.

LONG-RANGE PLANNING

Although our emphasis to date has been on the large banks handling sizable trades (because that's where the action is), the small investor in Europe is certainly an attractive candidate for long-range cultivation. Personal savings rates are unusually high, and the small investor's willingness to invest in U.S. securities was demonstrated by the successful selling record of Investors Overseas Services' mutual funds before that organization's much-publicized troubles. With the return of the small investor's confidence in U.S. investing, we're likely to see some positive changes in the investment profile of Europe.

Some chief executives schedule frequent visits overseas to conduct meetings or have luncheons with bankers and analysts, often coordinating these activities with visits to local facilities and other company business. The opportunity to gain exposure before investment groups and in financial and business journals is excellent, and the chief executive's involvement strengthens the credibility of a company's long-range program. It is wise not to visit more than once a year, however.

Japan is another area where interest in U.S. securities is mounting. Although Gillette has no firsthand experience in that country, its growing importance warrants at least a mention.

Restrictions on foreign investments there have been eased, and I'm told a number of prominent American companies are exploring the possibility of listing on the Tokyo Stock Exchange when final barriers have been lowered.

In view of Japan's chronic capital surpluses, a savings rate that is the highest in the world, and its interest in investing throughout the world, this may be the next place that U.S. corporations will rush to to become better known and to raise capital. Although the procedures for initiating an investor relations program there undoubtedly would be vastly different than in Europe, it is an area well worth investigating.

In summary the key points of any overseas investment relations program are these:

1. A proper introduction, or sponsorship, arranged through your U.S. investment banker or others who can lead you to the important institutions and decision makers.
2. Adequate planning and follow-through, and follow-up visits at least once each year.
3. Flexibility, so that your activities can be altered to fit the protocol and practices of each country you visit.
4. Recognition of the differences in how you will conduct your program in Europe as opposed to procedures in the United States.

And in closing, let me offer these tips that might make your visits a bit more productive, as well as comfortable.

1. If possible, take along a U.S. investment banker who can make practical suggestions on how the interviews are progressing and provide much other useful background information.

2. In your interviews, speak slowly and distinctly and avoid slang, colloquialisms, and uniquely American terms.

3. Always carry a suitable supply of the supporting materials you'll need—annual reports, factbooks, and so on —so that you can operate effectively if shipments are lost in transit.

4. If you don't know the local language, list the address of each appointment on a memo pad and give it to your driver.

5. Make a record of your meeting—including any comments from those who accompany you—as soon as possible after your appointment ends. I find that a portable tape recorder is a good way to record observations while they're fresh, and the tapes can be transcribed after my return to provide a full record. They also make good reference for my return the following year.

6. Always ask for the card of the persons you are talking with, as this may be the only way you can obtain the correct spelling of their name and their proper title for future correspondence.

Financial Press Relations

Robert B. Wolcott, Jr.

FINANCIAL PRESS RELATIONS and publicity are major elements of a comprehensive investor relations program. They are valuable because they provide unique and distinct opportunities to keep the public—and in particular the investing public—well informed of important corporate developments in a way not possible by personal contact or mailed material.

One of the most important ingredients in financial publicity is its role in handling fast-breaking spot news. No other medium of investor relations can get the comprehensive, accurate story of what happened to a corporation displayed before the general public, the company's stockholders, the financial community, and the press as quickly as can financial publicity. Examples of this capability are announcements of acquisitions or mergers, changes in divi-

Robert B. Wolcott, Jr., is Executive Vice President, Burson-Marsteller, Los Angeles, Calif.

dend policies, important executive appointments, sales and earnings statements, and major government contracts. In every instance the role of financial publicity is to get this news out fast, accurately, and broadly, and if done properly, it can be one of the most important parts of any company's investor relations program. Good financial publicity supplies that critical ingredient of instant communications that no other aspect of investor relations can provide.

THE FINANCIAL PRESS—A DESCRIPTION

The outlets for financial publicity are the following: the financial sections of major daily newspapers; a limited number of specialized daily financial–business newspapers; news magazines; specialized business and financial periodicals; the Dow Jones and Reuters news services, along with AP and UPI financial wires; the advisory and statistical services; and leading members of the trade press.

MAJOR DAILY NEWSPAPERS

Most daily newspapers in the twenty-five largest U.S. cities have a financial section, some no more than two pages in length, others quite extensive. Morning newspapers generally carry the most comprehensive financial news because their deadlines allow enough time for greater detail. The bulk of financial-section coverage involves stock listings— the New York, American, and regional exchanges, plus the National Association of Securities Dealers' list of over-the-counter stocks. Some smaller sections will carry a wire service–selected NYSE list of the largest and most actively traded securities, as limited space doesn't permit carrying the full listings.

In addition to various stock lists, financial sections also carry wire service stories on daily market activity and analyses; material supplied by their own reporters; and edited information received directly from corporations and public relations firms representing publicly held corporate clients.

In certain newspapers the financial section has its own daily columnist. Others run by-line commentaries provided by the wire services and syndicates. Photography is carried on a limited basis, mainly because space is not available. Sunday sections usually consist of mostly feature articles. The Saturday and Monday sections tend to be small, since the paper is less bulky on Saturday and on Monday there are no stock lists.

NATIONAL DAILY FINANCIAL NEWSPAPERS

The No. 1 publication in the field of specialized business and financial dailies is *The Wall Street Journal*. It has a daily circulation of well over a million copies and publishes four regional editions to permit fast, next-day distribution.

Besides offering complete coverage of corporate and security news, the *Journal* also runs important economic, financial, and political news and frequently publishes interesting, off-beat feature stories. Daily articles on the "Abreast of the Market" page frequently have had significant impact on the trading of both individual securities and certain industry categories, as have page one leader articles.

The *Journal* operates news bureaus in more than twenty major business and financial centers throughout the country. All the news material prepared by its correspondents is sent to the New York headquarters for editing and is then transmitted to the four regional-edition printing plants. The Eastern edition generally runs the largest issue because of its greater circulation and advertiser appeal. Although certain stories are required to run in all four editions, each individual regional editor has some flexibility regarding layout and use of other news material.

The Wall Street Journal policy on placement of news material is specific. Corporations are assigned to either the bureau in their own city or the bureau closest to it. It does not permit a company not based in New York City to place news material with the *Journal's* headquarters office, except, on occasion, when the news originates in New York City.

The other major national financial newspaper is the *New York Journal of Commerce*. This publication provides a somewhat different type of news coverage and places principal emphasis on commerce and trade. It is known particularly for its comprehensive coverage of news in the fields of insurance, textiles, chemicals, petroleum, foods, world trade, and shipping. Distribution mainly is in New York City, although copies are circulated nationally on a limited basis.

FINANCIAL NEWS SERVICES

There are two major specialized financial news services— Dow Jones and Reuters. In addition, Associated Press and United Press International have financial wires to supplement their general news services. Member papers of AP or UPI can obtain everything from exchange and NASD stock lists to a wide range of business and financial news.

The most important of these services is the Dow Jones. Monday through Friday, from 9 A.M. to 5:30 P.M., the

Dow Jones broad tape issues a steady stream of general and corporate information that is transmitted directly to financial institutions, many important newspapers, and offices of organizations interested in financial news. Those on the receiving end have Dow Jones equipment installed in their offices and receive tens of thousands of words a day on what is called the "broad tape," as distinguished from the narrower ticker, which carries just stock transactions.

The Dow Jones service is in a position to supply news of unusual comprehensiveness at great speed. This is significant because an important story, such a company's earnings or a merger, can be flashed across the country in a matter of minutes after it hits the Dow Jones desk in New York. This instant communication of information to brokerage houses can have an immediate effect on market action. Many afternoon newspapers find the Dow Jones service attractive, for its gives them an opportunity to carry financial news and final stock prices the same day.

In recent years the internationally famous Reuters news service has established a financial wire service in the United States and has become a vigorous competitor with Dow Jones. Its news is carried over a similar transmission system and received on modern machines in a large number of brokerage office locations around the country. It does not have nearly the coverage of Dow Jones, but it does possess a vigorous reporting force that constantly tries to gain the advantage over its much larger competitor.

Whereas the brokerage community relies heavily on the Dow Jones and Reuters news services for fast-breaking and critical financial information, most newspapers use material received from the Associated Press and United Press International. Between them, they cover all newspapers of any significant size. It is highly important, therefore, that any company's financial publicity program include placement with AP and UPI.

FINANCIAL PERIODICALS

Although *The Wall Street Journal,* the daily newspapers, and the wire services represent the absolutely essential media for a successful publicity operation, there are also a number of financial periodicals of importance. These do not provide extensive opportunities for the use of normal company news information, but they do carry market analyses and market-trend and investment-type information as well as profiles on individual corporations.

One of the most influential of these publications is *Barron's,* a weekly tabloid-size newspaper that is part of the Dow Jones organization. *Barron's* deals broadly with business and economic matters and carries industry- and economic-trend stories in its front section. From three to five individual corporate profiles also appear each week, plus a large statistical section. On page one, columnist Alan Abelson writes a weekly column that is widely read and often responsible for immediate market action. Probably no two publications in the country have a more direct bearing on changes in stock trading than *The Wall Street Journal* and *Barron's.*

Another leading financial periodical is *Forbes,* whose circulation now outstrips *Fortune*'s. This twice-a-month publication is written and edited in provocative style and is highly readable. Individual company stories are intermixed with articles on industries, and the publication also has several by-lined columnists.

Financial World is one of the oldest of the weekly financial periodicals. It deals broadly with market, economic, and industry matters and runs stories on individual corporations. A certain amount of current corporate news is carried in one of its sections, and the publication also regularly covers the mutual fund field. From time to time *Financial World* also carries a supplement with its own independent appraisals of listed companies. The publication has done much to upgrade the quality of annual reports by its annual awards competition.

Other periodicals in this field include the *Magazine of Wall Street,* whose content is similar to that of *Financial World.* The *Commercial and Financial Chronicle* is published semiweekly and is aimed directly at the investment community. *Investment Dealers' Digest* is published weekly and carries a great deal of information regarding registrations, security offerings, and items of special interest to brokerage firms. It is probably more closely oriented to the investment community than any other publication and in this respect resembles an industry trade periodical.

NEWS AND BUSINESS MAGAZINES

In addition to the highly specialized financial media, publications such as *Business Week, Fortune,* and *Dun's Review* are important targets for financial publicity.

Business Week carries an extensive amount of business and economic news. It is divided into a number of editorial departments, such as "Companies," "Management," "Marketing," "Finance," and "The Markets," and also runs industry roundup stories and individual corporate profiles.

From a prestige standpoint *Fortune* ranks high as an important national business magazine. Its industry and individual corporate stories usually are comprehensive in scope, but the average corporation finds it difficult to penetrate directly because its single-company profiles usually cover only the largest firms. The "Businessmen in the News" section, however, does represent an opportunity for placement of important corporate appointments.

Dun's is a monthly periodical covering general business subjects, management profiles, finance, executive compensation, personnel administration, and similar broad topics.

The weekly newsmagazines such as *Time* and *Newsweek* have sections devoted to business and finance and to economics. Large corporations can often rate attention by these publications, but for the most part the news they carry is related to the past week's developments and to overall trends. *U.S. News & World Report,* which is edited in Washington, D.C., runs some news of the business world, but its editorial policies are heavily weighted in favor of news coverage related to the government and developments emanating from the nation's capital.

THE TRADE PRESS

Leading trade publications merit some consideration because many of them are read by investment analysts. Examples of a few well-read industry publications are *Aviation Week & Space Technology, Women's Wear Daily, Electronic News,* and *Chemical and Engineering News.* The top trade journals, highly respected in their own industry fields, often are read by other editors in the business press as well as by investment analysts. To this degree they can be influential in a financial press relations program.

RADIO AND TELEVISION

No more than a decade ago, inclusion of electronic media in a financial publicity program would have rated a few chuckles. Today, however, a great deal of financial news is carried by radio and television, once again because of the enormous increase in public interest in corporate financial information.

Most business and financial news carried on radio news programs during the workweek concerns stock market trading activity. The Dow Jones industrial averages are well known today, thanks in good part to their frequent inclusion in hourly radio news programs. In certain major cities there are specialized business–financial radio shows that run from five to fifteen minutes. These cover the latest trading activity as well as important breaking business and financial news issued that day.

The television picture is somewhat spotty, although the final market averages often are carried on TV network and local station news programs. Certain cities have UHF television stations that are devoted to financial news; their audience is small, but it is highly selective, consisting primarily of corporate executives and members of the investment fraternity. These shows carry continuous viewing of the stock ticker, and some of them program interviews with corporate executives.

WORKING WITH THE FINANCIAL PRESS

Success in placing corporate financial publicity is usually a combination of newsworthy material and effective working relationships with the business and financial press. These relationships should be handled professionally, not by an individual whose training is in another discipline. Editors are sensitive human beings. They respect objective handling and will cooperate with financial publicists if dealt with on a consistent, fair, and informative basis.

The organization of a financial press relations program begins with the identification of the corporation's target audiences. First would be the major local newspapers in the headquarters city. Then come the business and financial media, usually in the order described above. Getting to know financial editors, correspondents, and bureau managers of important national media is essential—not just for the sake of friendly relations but, more importantly, to determine by personal contact their own ground rules, likes and dislikes, deadlines, and special requirements.

For the most part the average financial department of a daily newspaper is not large, and therefore one rarely finds reporters who specialize in covering a particular industry. This is not the case with a paper such as *The New York Times* or the New York staff of *The Wall Street Journal,* both of which have a number of reporters assigned as specialists for a given industry. Keep these individuals updated on your corporation's activities, so that when they write industry roundup stories, your company is automatically contacted, quoted, and appropriately included.

Financial news desks are flooded every day with news releases, wire service copy, and other material. Therefore, special steps should be taken by corporations, particularly small- and medium-size, to gain an identity. This can be done by preparing an information memorandum that covers the history, background, products, services, plants, management, and financial position of the company. This serves as a backdrop for subsequent news releases and positions the editor more knowledgeably on your company. The information can be supplemented by the annual stockholder report, the latest prospectus or proxy statement, and similar material designed to keep the media updated.

Another technique used in establishing good press relations is to introduce the chief executive officer to important financial editors. If it's a local newspaper, their financial editors should get to know your top officers, through periodic, individual backgrounding and discussion meetings. For corporations headquartered outside New York City, the chief executive officers should visit this national news center and be introduced personally to top media editors. This is especially important, for national publications often can overlook important companies simply for reasons of geographical distance.

FINANCIAL PUBLICITY AND HOW TO PLACE IT

Corporations often do things that are newsworthy and of general public interest. Examples are reports of sales and earnings, dividend actions, major financing efforts, mergers and acquisitions, major new products, new plants, technological or research breakthroughs, important executive speeches, annual stockholder meetings, and major personnel appointments.

On the other hand, many companies feel they have done things that merit news attention when clearly the event or action is of no news value at all. Those in charge of financial press relations should promptly and continually stress the difference between news and non-news. Nothing can disturb a financial press relations program more than for a company to issue a flood of puffy blurbs to an already-overworked news desk. This turns off editors, can damage good press relations, and makes it difficult for the company to get legitimate news placed thereafter.

Most corporate information is disseminated to the press in the form of news releases. Here are some suggestions for the preparation and placement of news material.

1. The news release should be professionally written, as close to newspaper style as possible. Copy should be double-spaced, with plenty of margin provided at the sides and top to allow room for editorial marking. Always include the name and telephone number of the company liaison for possible press contact.

2. News releases should be as comprehensive as possible. All important elements should be included, even when the news is unfavorable. Be succinct and concise. Lengthy, gushy quotes and flowery descriptions are not essential parts of the news release, and documents such as those usually are thrown away.

3. Arrange the facts in logical, meaningful order, so that it is easy to see at a glance what the real story involves. In the case of a merger story, what were the terms of the agreement—stock or cash? Which is the surviving company? What additional approvals are needed? These and other integral facts should be placed high in the story to give the editor at quick glance the significance of the transaction.

4. Make certain that your news releases go out as early in the day as possible. This allows the editors more time for checking and meeting early deadlines.

5. Send your news releases by messenger or by one of the commercial public relations wire services. Don't make

personal visits to editors unless the story clearly needs a good bit of verbal amplification. This can usually be done just as easily on the telephone.

6. Don't call the editor to find out if he's going to run the story, and don't call to find out why it didn't run. Editors are busy people and such bothersome calls can only diminish the effectiveness of your press relations program.

7. Don't call a press conference if a news release will suffice. A major editorial complaint over the years has been that too many non-news press conferences are held.

8. Be sure that inquiries from reporters on breaking news stories are handled rapidly and accurately. Access to top management for answers to press questions is essential; otherwise the story may not run or will run in incomplete or inaccurate form.

9. Again, bad news rates the same professional treatment as good news. Consistency pays off with editors. Don't try to hide unfavorable news.

Distribution of news releases can be handled in several ways. Messenger service is reliable and fast and has the advantage of getting to the right person. There also are several commercial public relations newswire services that provide instant coverage of most of the important financial publications throughout the country. PR Newswire is one of these services. Corporate news releases are run verbatim on their own equipment, and usually this information is taken off the teleprinter at the individual publication and placed on the financial desk. Utilization of this service helps immeasurably in providing full and immediate disclosure of financial information, since it reaches all news media at the same time. These commercial wire services also cover a large number of brokerage houses with the same information. The advantage of this service is that the complete company release is distributed, not just an edited wire service excerpt. Since these services cover all major cities, the need to mail news releases and the risk of varying delivery dates are eliminated. However, distribution can be supplemented by mail to cover weekly and monthly publications where arrival time is not as critical.

Always be selective in your distribution. Great sums of money are wasted annually because tremendous numbers of news releases are sent to the wrong places. Setting up a mailing list of all the daily newspapers in the United States and sending them all your news releases is absolutely the wrong way to proceed. The financial editor of a paper in Georgia could hardly be interested in news of an assistant sales manager appointed in a Seattle office. Such distribution procedures not only waste the company's money but irritate the editor who has to handle the worthless releases.

In addition to the placement of normal corporate news, financial publicity can include the development of feature articles and corporate profiles. These don't run frequently, but when they do, they focus maximum attention on a company.

In order to obtain these special articles, the financial press relations practitioner first must know his targets. He should know what kind of material the individual publication runs. Nothing can be more wasteful than to send the right story idea to the wrong publication.

Financial sections of many large daily newspapers occasionally will run feature articles during the week, but those that have Sunday sections are more inclined to schedule them there.

The best approach is to prepare a concise, well-organized story outline tailored to the individual publication's editorial requirements. If this suggestion is accepted, then the next step usually is an interview with a top corporate officer. Background information should be supplied in advance so that the reporter is well armed by the time the interview takes place.

In working with major national publications, the usual procedure for the financial press relations practitioner is to contact the bureau in the city where the company is headquartered. Most national media do not like story ideas submitted directly to New York headquarters if they have a bureau in your particular city. If the company is headquartered in New York, then contact often can be made through an individual reporter who covers your industry.

IMPORTANT GOVERNMENT REGULATIONS

In recent years, the importance of financial publicity has increased largely because of the growing emphasis placed by the Securities and Exchange Commission on full and timely disclosure of "material" information. The famous *Texas Gulf Sulphur* case represents a historic benchmark decision regarding liability and insider trading. Failure to release material information can now bring both regulatory and court action leading to heavy penalties. No longer can a few individuals with access to privileged information use such confidential data to trade stocks to their own personal advantage. The result of court decisions and regulatory actions has been a greater flow of material information to the nation's business and financial press. These crucial developments also have placed a greater burden on those responsible for financial press relations, as well as on corporate management itself, to make certain that full and timely disclosure requirements are consistently met. The practitioner, therefore, should become knowledgeable about these requirements, court decisions, and regulatory actions in his own self-interest.

One of the problems created by the great increase in the number of publicly held companies and the consequent upsurge in financial information released to the press is the growing inability of the nation's newspapers to provide enough space to carry all of this news. In the financial sections of most daily newspapers, the preponderant amount of space is devoted to various stock lists. In many cases, less than 10 percent of the available space is used for news material. This means that many corporations find that their important financial information is either not carried at all, runs in agate type, or is carried only in publications with enough space, like *The Wall Street Journal*. This has placed many corporations and their financial press relations people in a serious dilemma. If material information is released but doesn't appear in print, is this a violation of full and timely disclosure? The SEC has understood their plight and considers the full release of news material to press services and by mailings as an exemplification of good faith.

The field of financial press relations continues to be one of the integral parts of a well-conducted investor relations program. The benefits to be obtained from organizing and conducting an informative press relations program can be considerable. Assuming good company performance, development of good rapport with financial editors means that newsworthy stories, generally speaking, will get the space they deserve. Acceptance of feature article proposals is another example of where knowledge of the company and good press relations can pay off, and automatic inclusion in industry roundup stories is yet another telltale piece of evidence.

The investing climate today has changed dramatically. A full and free flow of information no longer is a choice for corporate management. Therefore, it seems only logical to see that the financial press relations aspect of the investor relations program is well organized, conducted professionally, and handled with great objectivity.

PART II

Case Histories

Kaufman and Broad

Barbara Sayre Casey

AMONG 763 companies listed on the New York Stock Exchange in 1972, Kaufman and Broad, Inc., enjoyed the greatest growth in common stock value in the five years from 1968 to 1972—a spectacular 1,153 percent increase, according to *Forbes* magazine. This performance in the market must be attributed to three major factors: the company's exceptional growth record, its highly respected management team, and the investment community's great interest in housing during some of those years.

However, the company's thoughtfully conceived, carefully planned, and well-executed investor relations program also must be credited with a significant, if small, role.

Kaufman and Broad was founded in Detroit in 1957 with $25,000 by Eli Broad, then twenty-three years old and a recently certified public accountant, and Donald

Barbara Sayre Casey is Vice President, Corporate Relations, Kaufman and Broad, Inc., Los Angeles, Calif.

Kaufman, then thirty-four and a home remodeling contractor.

Sixteen years later, the company had sales of $284 million, a net income of $19.9 million, capitalization of $176 million, and a market value of about $600 million. Its growth propelled it to being the country's largest multinational housing producer, with operations throughout the United States and in Canada, France, and Germany.

A record like this could not be ignored in the marketplace. But it was supported by three definite advantages:

1. Strong credibility based on consistent performance, credibility that cannot be developed by any other means.
2. Management that considers communication with 100 percent of shareholders as a responsibility of heading a public company. Both Chairman Broad and President Eugene S. Rosenfeld firmly believe that keeping shareholders informed and building investor confidence is part of the job shareholders rightfully expect from a public company's management.
3. Professional investor relations that helped secure proper recognition and response for the company and its record.

Kaufman and Broad's initial public offering came in 1961. There was only one other public homebuilder at that time, but Mr. Broad, perceiving that only a public company would be able to secure the capital, management, and reputation to achieve his long-term goals, convinced Bache & Co. to underwrite an offering.

Kaufman and Broad became the first housing company to be listed on the American Stock Exchange. That was in

1962. At that time, the company moved its headquarters to Los Angeles. It had no formal investor relations program from 1961 until I joined the company in June 1967. Prior to this, the financial public relations efforts had been supervised by the executive vice president, who was in charge of writing the annual and quarterly reports and issuing mandatory news releases.

Mr. Broad possessed an innate sense of financial public relations, and he personally had achieved some recognition through meetings with analysts and addresses to security analyst societies. There had never been a planned, consistent program with clearly established goals.

In mid-1967, Mr. Broad and I, in a series of lengthy meetings, reviewed short- and long-term corporate goals, which we then used as a basis to formulate a formal investor relations program. These meetings, held at the end of each year, have continued over the past five years. However, we do meet informally from time to time throughout the year to evaluate our performance and to shift our program as corporate goals and a changing environment dictate.

We do not create an entirely new program each year. Sometimes only refinements are made.

In the five years 1967 to 1972, we implemented three basic investor relations strategies:

1. Gaining recognition within the investment community for Kaufman and Broad and the new housing industry.
2. Utilizing housing's "glamour" years.
3. Establishing Kaufman and Broad as a growth company.

GAINING RECOGNITION

Before we could begin gaining recognition within the invest-ment community for Kaufman and Broad, it was obvious that we had to find a way to distinguish us from the rest of the homebuilding industry. (Homebuilders had a poor image with everyone in the financial community. They were regarded as unstable, financially unsound, and unprofes-sionally managed.)

During the severe credit crunches of 1966 and 1967, many small homebuilders experienced bad times, some even going out of business. However, the larger, professionally managed, and well-financed housing companies, Kaufman and Broad among them, continued to achieve record sales and earnings. This was definitely a story that we needed to tell Wall Street. Thus, a major aim of our initial investor relations program was to disassociate ourselves from "home-building" and to create recognition for a new breed of housing company.

The story of the new housing industry led by Kaufman and Broad, which was emerging as a new force in Ameri-can business, became a vital part of all our communica-tions. We repeated it in literature and speeches, in formal and informal presentations. We emphasized the differences between the professional housing producer and the typical small homebuilder. These differences are summarized in our business practices, which were created by Mr. Broad at the time of the company's founding and have continued ever since. These policies have been the backbone of the company's steady growth and the prototype for all large companies in the housing industry. They include treating land as a raw material, producing homes after sale, main-taining a manufacturing orientation, financing inventory from capital funds, arranging customer mortgages in advance, diversifying geographically, and decentralizing management.

In addition to mobilizing our investor relations and public relations efforts to communicate this story, we felt we could more successfully and rapidly reach our goal if we enlisted other members of the new housing industry. Therefore, in early 1968 we initiated formation of an organization called the Council of Housing Producers. We gathered together twelve of the largest housing producers in the United States and discussed our common problems. We realized that the giant National Association of Home Builders, representing more than fifty thousand independent homebuilders, generally did not uphold the viewpoint of the large housing producer and that we were unknown to the press, the government, and Wall Street.

The Council of Housing Producers was essentially a public relations and lobbying organization, but it filled a definite vacuum in the housing industry and quickly gained credibility as its spokesman. Overnight the new housing industry became an accepted reality.

Once this was accomplished, we moved into phase two: gaining recognition for Kaufman and Broad as the leader of the new housing industry. We began to tell the growth story of the company, which was not generally well known in the investment community. Our program started with the development of a list of influential persons within the investment community whom we wanted to reach. These were primarily the security analysts at brokerage firms and institutions who specialized in various aspects of building or construction. At this time, there were no analysts assigned specifically to housing. Analysts generally followed the building materials companies, real estate development firms, or companies in the general category of construction.

It is my firm belief that the key to success in any investor relations program is a good mailing list. Kaufman and Broad previously had one that was incomplete and out of date. Our first task was to organize a list of large shareholders, key analysts who might follow Kaufman and Broad, appropriate government officials, bankers, vendors, and other very important "publics."

After developing this list, we realized we had a scarcity of communications vehicles. We had begun to issue more than just the mandatory news releases, and we sent the most important of these to our mailing list. But we still needed other, more informal communications vehicles.

As part of our initial public relations program, we had created a quarterly employee publication called *Spectrum,* which we also sent to our bankers, vendors, government officials, and others with whom we did business. Because of the far-flung nature of our company, its youth, and its high percentage of management personnel, *Spectrum* was not a typical house organ. Its contents were company plans and activities, product and people stories, human interest features, and editorials about company positions on major issues. *Spectrum* was well received by our employees, who liked being informed about all of Kaufman and Broad's activities, not just those in their territory, and by other publics who received it. Some shareholders and analysts asked to be placed on the mailing list, and so we increased *Spectrum*'s circulation to include these audiences as well.

The next step in our investor relations program was person-to-person meetings with analysts, shareholders, and investment counselors, as well as small group meetings of analysts and shareholders. Key executives spoke to appropriate analyst society splinter groups.

We also sought speaking dates before security analyst societies to circulate our message to as many people as possible and to provide a forum for publicity. In 1968 we spoke to the New York and San Francisco security analyst societies and reprinted these talks, distributing them nationally to our mailing list and to all who requested information on the company.

Analysts were encouraged to visit the company to meet and talk with senior officers and to tour our housing communities in Southern California.

We measured our success after the first year by the interest shown in our company: requests for information, number of analyst visits, requests for speaking dates, and the number of analyst research reports recommending purchase of the company's shares.

A third level of communications of our initial program was boosting housing's prospects. We forecast a housing boom for the 1970s unlike any in our country's history. Our efforts were soon strengthened by in-depth reports on housing's future growth by analysts, economists, and the government.

Utilizing Housing's Glamour Years

With the pending housing boom and the increasing interest in public housing companies by brokerage firms, institutional shareholders, and the financial community in 1969 and 1970, we changed our program to reinforce Kaufman and Broad's position as the leader of this fast-growing industry.

A major part of this effort was press relations. We worked at becoming known to the local and national media and at being thought of synonymously with housing. A story appeared in *Business Week* in 1970, and Kaufman and Broad was one of the few small companies ever to be featured in *Fortune*. At every opportunity we told the press why housing was the new "glamour" industry; we gave them the important statistics and encouraged them to write stories on housing's potential and how, combined with the rise of professional housing producers, it would be the most exciting industry in the United States in the 1970s.

Housing's glamour years were 1970 and 1971; investors placed high values on housing and housing-related companies. In fact, they seemed willing to pay almost anything for unproved modular housing companies. Kaufman and Broad withstood great investor pressure to enter the modular housing industry during this time. Our research indicated that the country was not technologically, economically, or psychologically ready for modular housing, and we firmly maintained this position. We since have been proved correct.

During 1970 and 1971, a chief consideration in our planning was how to continue our investor relations program yet not seem promotional. The company was glamorized by a growing corps of housing analysts. Therefore, we told our story as simply as possible. We were careful not to become slick but maintained our usual "look" in communications and our usual frugality in expenditures.

ESTABLISHING KAUFMAN AND BROAD
AS A GROWTH COMPANY

Although we were riding a wave of popularity in 1971, we foresaw that housing was going to become "last year's story" in 1972. Housing starts had become the gauge of our industry—and we knew they would not climb forever. Thus, we again shifted the direction of our investor relations program. Our goal became to establish Kaufman and Broad as a strong, professionally run company with an excellent growth record and an equally good future, not a company which grows only in boom housing years.

We stressed the fact that our company's growth had not been, was not then, and would not become dependent upon the growth of the housing industry. This message appeared prominently in our written communications to shareholders, in speeches, and in personal meetings with shareholders and analysts. We used graphics extensively to contrast our record with housing's ups and downs, showing that our company had been able to grow in both good and bad housing years.

Although 1972 was again a record for housing, the luster began to fade as investors indicated worry about a future decline in housing starts. In the best housing year in history there was a noticeable weakening of investor confidence.

We continued to emphasize our basic growth story, expanding it to include our major competitive strengths: multinational operations, proven management, and a financial services group.

We also stepped up a program to call on our large shareholders, which we had inaugurated in 1970. The program was handled informally: we would schedule an hour's visit to one or two shareholders by a senior executive when he was in a certain city. This proved to be extremely successful; attendance was generally good at these meetings and our executives received a warm reception.

In these meetings, one executive would make a brief talk, covering timely points or those we thought to be of special concern to the investor, and then would answer questions.

We believe that good communications helped maintain confidence and loyalty during the second half of 1972 and the beginning of 1973, a period of declining performance by building and housing stocks. Management calls continue to be part of our investor relations program.

How We Treat Analysts

When we began our investor relations program in 1967, we established an open-door policy. In keeping with management's commitment to shareholder communications, the president and chairman of our company are available, which has been an important boost to our efforts. Both men are extremely cooperative and are available to talk with people, attend meetings, or make presentations whenever I commit them.

Our policy toward visits was informal at first. Several of our staff visited with analysts, and we usually gave them a personal tour of our local housing developments. As our following grew, this activity became unrealistic and time-consuming. Therefore, we formalized our policy and limited visits to an hour and a half for each analyst: an hour with me or another vice president, then thirty minutes with the chairman, president, or operating group head.

We investigated the possibility of holding joint analyst meetings on certain days of the month. However, after interviewing companies that followed this method, some that did not, and our own analysts, we decided this was not consistent with our open-door policy.

We also established a policy of excluding visits with our

line executives, since it consumed too much of their valuable time. However, our program is set up to provide opportunities for analysts to meet with these important people. Since 1970, we have arranged annual analyst tours of one of our on-site housing divisions. We invite our North American housing managers to join these tours, as well as all department heads of the division where we are visiting. Thus analysts have an opportunity to meet and talk with these important line managers. And they can ask many of the nitty-gritty questions that we in the corporate office can't keep up on daily.

When we speak to security analyst groups or to small meetings in different cities, line managers located in the area attend along with the corporate officer who is speaking. This again permits analysts to meet these very key people.

We also follow the same policy for analysts that we follow for the press: to handle every call and request as promptly as possible, considering the needs and deadlines of the caller, and to be honest. When I don't know an answer, I simply say so. Or, when policy forbids disclosing information, I forthrightly explain the situation. We try to keep in mind what an analyst needs to serve his company or clients. For example, we make sure that he receives annual reports, news releases, and so on as soon as his clients.

WHAT MAKES OUR INVESTOR RELATIONS WORK?

Kaufman and Broad is proof that a company can achieve sophisticated investor relations goals with a small budget and staff. For three years my staff consisted of me and a secretary, but I was able to call on various other people in the company to assist with analyst contacts and special projects. Mr. Broad was an invaluable contributor to strategy and planning.

In 1970 we added a writer–editor, promoted the secretary to administrative assistant with responsibility for mailings, printing, scheduling, and so forth, and added a secretary. We now are expanding the staff further to include a communications director and a researcher.

Our annual budget for all corporate communications, including investor relations, started at $63,353 in 1968 and grew to $125,000 in 1972. These figures also included salaries.

Success does not rest on numbers—either of people or of dollars. Certainly you must have competent people who utilize dollars well. But it's my opinion that five factors have been primary in our success: management commitment, planning, consistency, sensitivity, and credibility.

MANAGEMENT COMMITMENT

Management commitment is foremost. An investor relations genius could not implement a successful program without it. Management must believe in the program, support it, and display respect for the investor relations professional both within and outside the company. This management support is reflected in the attitude of a company's financial publics. For example, analysts often remark that they feel confident in talking with me because they know I am totally informed about the company, its plans, goals, and activities. People you work with regularly are sensitive to your relationship with management and your place in the company.

Our management also discusses potential major business decisions with me. My reaction, based on sensitivity to our publics, helps management to evaluate its decisions. In addition, by being informed early of its plans, I have sufficient time to develop potential strategy for any action.

Wall Street hates surprises, even a nice one. That is the first thing to be learned by anyone in investor relations. A company may be forgiven almost anything—but only if it is *not* a surprise. Any type of startling news sprung on the financial community brings major repercussions. Therefore, it is important for you to be informed early of possible activities or decisions and to take appropriate steps for communications.

PLANNING

Whether it's formal or informal, successful investor relations requires some type of regular planning. Basic strategy should be defined and a program devised to implement it. Our planning generally is on an informal basis, usually written down by me in a yellow tablet. What is important is that we know what we are trying to achieve. We evaluate our planning frequently, and we feel free to revise and shift, partly because it is not set down in a hundred-page printed piece.

CONSISTENCY

Skillful security analysts develop antennae to sense subtleties in the companies they follow. Any change in policy or attitude is picked up, examined, and analyzed for hidden meanings. Consequently, consistency of style is highly important in any investor relations program.

From the beginning, we determined that we would have an open-door policy to analysts. Although we have had no down earnings since then, we have experienced bad news and other negative events. Yet we have continued our policy without any variance and have always been available to analysts, attempting to answer their questions with as much honesty as possible.

Other companies have been successful with a closed-door investor relations program. I disagree with this approach philosophically, but a company that chooses this position should pursue it consistently.

SENSITIVITY

Investor relations people need to develop antennae, too. Sensitivity to others—their needs, their drives, their body language—pays valuable dividends. Often it is not what is said that is meaningful but what is unsaid.

Sensitivity to others wins confidence, enabling you to better convey your message to the outside and to receive feedback. And providing management with feedback is a valuable byproduct of investor relations. It can mean the difference between success and failure for a business decision.

CREDIBILITY

This is what it all boils down to. But there are so many credibility gaps in business today that it's an awesome task to build a bridge.

Time and performance build credibility. If you say something, you must do it. A multiple is not built on broken promises. At Kaufman and Broad, our policy is never to announce an action or a plan until we are 100 percent confident that it will be consummated. Along the way we may pass up public relations bonanzas, but we believe the long-term goal is more important than the short-term gain.

The fact that we have performed consistently has given us a credibility base with our shareholders and financial publics on which we can build in future years.

Winnebago Industries

Lawrence N. Crail

THE INVESTOR RELATIONS PROGRAMS of most public companies, whether listed on one or more stock exchanges or traded over the counter, are intended to maintain a fair market price for the companies' securities in an orderly and stable market. What constitutes a "fair" price for the stock is of course subject to varying perspectives. Moreover, maintenance of an orderly and stable market for securities becomes difficult when the company is in a rapid growth phase in a "glamour" industry that draws investors like a magnet.

Winnebago Industries, Inc., of Forest City, Iowa, was founded in 1958 to provide jobs in an economically depressed agricultural area of northern Iowa. The company has grown rapidly and today is the nation's leading manufacturer of recreational vehicles, including motor homes,

Lawrence N. Crail is Manager, Investor Relations, Winnebago Industries, Inc., Forest City, Iowa.

travel trailers, pickup camper coaches, "fifth wheel" trailers, and pickup truck covers, or Kaps®. The category recreational vehicles does *not* include such products as snowmobiles, all-terrain vehicles, dune buggies, or four-wheel-drive vehicles.

Because both the above categories of vehicle could properly be called recreational, the group with which Winnebago Industries is identified is increasingly referred to as "recreational shelter" vehicles. Another area of confusion in the minds of investors as well as others is the similarity in name between motor homes and mobile homes. Mobile homes, of course, are low-cost housing, and therefore certainly provide shelter, but they are not self-propelled and are a good deal less *mobile* than are motor homes. Motor homes are self-contained, self-propelled vehicles designed to provide living accommodations while traveling.

The frequent confusion between motor homes and mobile homes, as well as the fact that some mobile home producers also build recreational vehicles, has led to a tendency for many investors mentally to group stocks of companies from both industries into one category. As a result, when news about one or the other group is announced, stock of companies in both categories tends to react.

The recreational-vehicle industry can be likened today to the automobile industry of fifty or so years ago, when there were about seven hundred separate and distinct manufacturers of automobiles in the United States. In the recreational-vehicle industry of today, there are approximately a thousand manufacturers of a diverse group of products. Probably fewer than a hundred of these manufacturers are producers of motor homes. Many of the companies in the industry are small and poorly capitalized. Industry leaders and a number of specialized analysts have said that as the growth in the industry begins to slow sometime in the future, competition will force many of the smaller companies to merge, be acquired, or simply go out of business. Because of the highly fragmented nature of the industry, it would be easy for the casual observer to be bewildered by the multiplicity of brand names and model names, as well as by the varying qualities of product available to him. Sophisticated investors, however, know that there are perhaps a dozen or fifteen manufacturers that are well managed, have at least adequate facilities, are sufficiently capitalized, and have the marketing organizations necessary to survive in what will become an increasingly competitive industry.

Some of the companies involved are "independents," whose sole business is manufacturing and selling recreational vehicles. Winnebago leads this group. Others are divisions of conglomerates or diversified companies whose primary businesses are in some field other than recreational vehicles. Thus, while the total corporation in many instances is larger than Winnebago, those entities whose sole business is recreational vehicles are all smaller than Winnebago.

The first public sale of Winnebago stock took place in January 1966 and was largely restricted to employees and friends of the company in the home community and surrounding area. Subsequent public offerings helped gain wider distribution of the company's stock, but a majority—even today—is held in Forest City.

In September 1970, the common stock of Winnebago Industries was listed on the New York Stock Exchange. Less than a month later, the investor relations department was established in order to meet the needs for investor information being generated by the expanding company and to project Winnebago to the financial community nationally on a continuing basis.

The investor relations department formulated these communications objectives: (1) to emphasize Winnebago's growth, product acceptance, fiscal strength, and emergence as a dominant force in an industry known for its many small, underfinanced companies, and (2) to delineate the expanding market for motor homes, Winnebago's progress in assembling a management team and professional sales force, and the development of the manufacturing facilities necessary to meet the increasing demand for the company's products.

Winnebago has a very positive story to tell in comparison with its competitors. Most producers of recreational vehicles, even today, are little more than assemblers. They buy components ready-made from many sources and merely put them together.

Winnebago, on the other hand, is more highly vertically integrated—in other words, manufactures from raw materials, or adds considerable value to, more of its own parts and pieces—than any other company in the recreational vehicle industry. Because Winnebago adds more value to its products, it is able to eliminate more of the suppliers' profits and thus can provide the retail customer with more value for his dollar expended on the product. Moreover, it is able to enjoy better profit margins for its shareholders. As a result, while many manufacturers in the industry are producing a 5 or 6 percent net earnings figure after taxes (as a percent of sales), Winnebago has been averaging somewhat higher than that for the past several years.

A quick study of the company's growth profile shows that as recently as 1966, sales were under $4.5 million. In the fiscal year ending February 24, 1973, sales exceeded $200 million. Winnebago became No. 1 in its industry by being in the right place at the right time with the right product—and by making the right decisions a majority of the time.

As one result, Winnebago management has become properly self-confident. A self-confident management is more likely to say yes when asked to increase its level of corporate disclosure. And, of course, it becomes even easier when the numbers are good. The Winnebago investor relations department operates on the belief that all investors, and potential investors as well, should have equal access to information likely to affect an investment decision. Obviously, not all investors will make the same use of information, but if all have it, and at the same time, at least they start from the same place—much as in a horse race.

An investor relations department that is armed with good, positive information to impart, a self-confident management willing to innovate, and a desire to establish stability in the market for the stock has an excellent atmosphere in which to communicate.

The usual means of communicating with the investment community are available to all companies: news releases on events of significance; quarterly reports to shareholders; meetings with securities analysts; interviews with financial news media; advertisements directed to the financial community; use of reprints of interviews, ads, and speeches. These are but a few, and Winnebago has used all of them.

What we have also done, and it has tickled the imagination of those who have heard about it, was to be the first company ever to send its 10-K form to all shareholders. We did this for the first time in the spring of 1971 and repeated it in 1972. It was a separate mailing from the annual report or proxy statement/notice of annual meeting. Exhibit 1 is the covering letter we drafted for the president's signature to explain to shareholders why they were receiving the company's 10-K. The 10-K is the formal annual report of a company to the Securities and Exchange Commission. Winnebago chose to take this pioneering step on the rather simplistic theory that once the 10-K is filed with the SEC it becomes public information available to anyone who wants to get it. It does contain considerable information not available through other routine sources, but the average shareholder does not have access to that information. He or she probably doesn't even know that it is available in a 10-K, or indeed, what a 10-K is. Thus, Winnebago's decision to send the 10-K to all shareholders was simply in the best interests of giving equal access to information to all investors and potential investors in Winnebago stock.

With the spring 1971 mailing of the first 10-K to shareholders, Winnebago sent a business reply card asking shareholders what they thought of the idea. Nearly a third of all shareholders of record responded affirmatively, with only a very few indicating they felt it was wasted effort or money. Here are a few of the comments:

This is a wonderful idea—adds real credibility to your company. 10-K reports are very inconvenient to obtain.—Washington analyst

Excellent idea—supplies all the material on the company—hope it starts a trend.—Philadelphia analyst

Very good. It strengthens my confidence in the company.—New York stockholder

Great idea. I'm suspicious of slick reports.—Illinois stockholder

An excellent idea.—New York analyst

Dissemination is a plus factor.—Boston analyst

Exhibit 1. Winnebago's statement on Form 10-K.

May 14, 1971

To the Shareholders of Winnebago Industries, Inc.

In 1968, we at Winnebago had our first public stock offering registered with the Securities and Exchange Commission. Every year since then we have had to file all sorts of information in Washington. Last year we listed our stock on the New York and Midwest Stock Exchanges. That meant more documents to be prepared and more places to file them. As a result, we now devote much time and effort to the presentation of information. We aren't complaining—just stating the facts of life which hold true for every publicly held corporation.

Now we read in the financial press that ". . . many companies obviously prefer to have the figures squirreled away in an SEC file cabinet rather than disseminated in thousands of stockholder reports." As with many things that anyone at Winnebago reads, that set us to thinking—

> Do we want to squirrel away any information?
>> Emphatically no.
> Are we?
>> We don't think so. We believe that nobody—not even the SEC—should have more information than our shareholders. We know that we are not "squirreling away" any information; the problem is to prove it.
> Why not give our shareholders exactly the same information we send to the SEC and the Exchanges?
>> Good idea—let's give it a try.

A copy of Winnebago's "Form 10-K" for this year is enclosed. The 10-K is every public company's annual report to the SEC; of all of the required filings, it is the most complete, and probably the most important. The 10-K isn't colorful like an annual report to shareholders, and there aren't any pictures. But the words and numbers tell a very full story about Winnebago.

We know of no other company that has distributed its 10-K to its shareholders. We want to know your reaction to our experiment. Enclosed is a postage-paid card that we would appreciate your returning to tell us whether or not you find this material helpful. What you have to say will help us decide whether to continue sending similar reports in the future.

Sincerely,

JOHN K. HANSON
President

Excellent move. I am impressed.—Pittsburgh broker

Excellent step forward.—San Francisco analyst

This is a terrific idea that more companies should follow.—New York broker

Excellent. "Just the facts."—Cincinnati broker

I like this concept very much.—Chicago analyst

I own stock in thirty companies and this is the best idea any have put forth.—Iowa stockholder

Great idea for the small individual investor who otherwise wouldn't see this information.—Illinois stockholder

Wonderful step forward. I hope the idea spreads.—Cincinnati broker

Great! Simply great idea! Plus, you've saved me the $3–$5 cost of getting the 10-K from the SEC.—Tennessee broker

As usual, Winnebago is a leader. I've read through the 10-K thoroughly and I've never known this much about a major company before.—Oklahoma stockholder

You have nothing to hide. An informed public is a confident public. Excellent.—Minnesota stockholder

Fantastic. I will personally do my best to bring your precedent to the attention of every company management I analyze.—California analyst

A great step forward for investment research. If only more U.S. corporations were as honorable.—Missouri stockholder

Outstanding idea—more companies should do it.—Chicago analyst

I think it is one of the finest stockholder relations moves I have ever seen.—Pittsburgh broker

Why not just send the 10-K to all shareholders and the investment community in place of the annual report and save the duplication of cost and effort? Indeed, in 1972 at least one company did just that, with only a covering letter.

While the 10-K is chock-full of information, it is not very beautiful. And if you want to paint a rosy picture, appeal to the pocketbook of the stockholder as a potential customer, or tell everyone of some of the activities about which you are particularly proud, then you need an instrument with which to do it. There is no question that in the not too distant future annual reports to shareholders and to the SEC will begin to look a great deal more alike and to contain essentially the same information.

Because this is inevitable, and because Winnebago has established a leadership position in communications to shareholders and the investment community, the company decided to combine its annual report to shareholders and the 10-K for the fiscal year ending in February 1973. That document took the form of a single cover with the contents double-bound inside. The annual report, containing the management letter and the report of operations, along with lots of pretty pictures, was supplemented by the more spartan-looking 10-K form, which served as the financial exhibits and legal report.

Another attempt to provide better communications with the financial community through a visual medium was the use of color photographs of Winnebago products in a stock offering prospectus. Boston Gas Company is believed to have been the first company in recent years to use color photographs in a prospectus, but the photos were of facilities rather than products. Winnebago's reasoning behind putting color pictures in the prospectus was that they would give the reader a quick identification of what the company's products were—again, to help the reader differentiate between motor homes and mobile homes.

Also, this prospectus, which was issued in December 1971, contained a "Mother Goose," or very simplified, summary of the offering that anyone could understand, in addition to the more complex legal language normally associated with prospectuses.

Winnebago was just starting to prepare its prospectus on its 1971 common stock offering when the SEC came out with a rules amendment suggesting the use of photographs, charts, and other graphic devices that would make such documents more understandable. This fit the company's communications philosophy perfectly, and the prospectus was prepared along the lines the SEC suggested.

The prospectus was sent to shareholders, financial editors, and the financial community, not only to provide them with the stock offering details, but also to give them updated information on the company and its performance.

In its mailing of the prospectus to financial editors and to the financial community, Winnebago said: "Our intent it to tell our story as clearly as we can to all those who are interested in Winnebago and its products."

And, in his covering letter to all shareholders receiving the prospectus, board chairman John V. Hanson said, in part: "We believe that our Prospectus is the most up-to-the-minute progress report available about Winnebago, and you, as shareholders, deserve to share the information it contains. We intend to have the best-informed shareholders in the country."

When the National Investor Relations Institute met in Washington for its 1971 annual convention, Alan B. Levenson, director of the division of corporate finance of the SEC, remarked before the group:

> As you know, the SEC has taken certain steps to achieve effective disclosure by trying to improve the readability of prospectuses. . . .
>
> I'd like to show what can be and has been done if there's a bona fide intent to communicate. Winnebago

Industries—listed on the New York Stock Exchange, by the way—which is the only company that sends all its shareholders the Commission's 10-K, recently filed a prospectus underwritten by Dean Witter. The second page contains a picture of its product in color. Thereafter, there is a prospectus summary using a columnar presentation, captions, short sentences, bar charts, and statistical data.

This progress toward readability, toward the visual approach to disclosure, toward short sentences, toward a readable document, must continue. Initiative should and must be encouraged, and we intend to do our part to see that it happens.

Winnebago common stock was listed on the New York Stock Exchange in September 1970. In the first full calendar year after its listing, in 1971, Winnebago was the leading gainer on the Exchange, with an increase in market price of over 460 percent. Coupled with the performance of the stock was a high level of visibility for the company as a result of attention by national television networks, news services, and magazines, as well as by many of these same media on a regional and local scale.

Because of Winnebago's very high profile during those years, the company has been visited by approximately 180 different securities analysts from the time its stock was first listed until the spring of 1973. And, just getting to Forest City, Iowa, is no small task.

To help avoid the disclosure problems associated with one-to-one conversations with securities analysts, Winnebago decided to expand its disclosure of information; at the same time, it set out to establish a system of controls in order to maintain a fair and orderly market in the securities of Winnebago Industries.

In the fall of 1972, the company sent a letter to its

financial mailing list in which recipients were asked to outline what information they believed they needed in order
to analyze Winnebago and the recreational-vehicle industry.
Exhibit 2 contains the text of that letter. While reactions
to it were mixed, a majority of the analysts responding felt
the letter was a good move. Some, however, interpreted it
to mean that Winnebago would be disclosing less information than in the past.

Exhibit 2. Winnebago's statement on information disclosure.

September 6, 1972

What would you like to know about Winnebago and/or the RV
industry? We feel it is time for a change in the manner of reporting of information that *you* want to know.

Frankly, we think you need more information about this
industry, in order to do your critical job of weighing and assessing,
comparing and deciding. We don't take our jobs lightly, and we
don't take yours lightly, either.

As a public company, we have an obligation to the investing
public to give that entire public a fair shot at pertinent information that could influence investment decisions. But we need your
help.

Effective immediately, Winnebago will not discuss weekly
production levels, retail and wholesale inventories, order backlogs,
or unit shipments. Instead, we will periodically publish selected
statistics, with explanatory text, so that everyone will have the
same information on which to base a decision at the same time.
What you do with it is up to you.

But we need to know what you want to know. And how often
you think you need it. Maybe we'll start a trend in the RV industry
that others will have to follow. Won't that help you?

Please give me your comments in writing as soon as possible.

Sincerely,

LAWRENCE N. CRAIL
Manager, Investor Relations

And, indeed, on a selective basis that was true. Winnebago began telling less to individual analysts on a one-to-one basis. However, on an overall, tell-the-world basis, Winnebago began giving more hard information to the entire investment community and to all its shareholders than either it or anyone else in the industry had ever given.

The letter clearly states Winnebago's underlying philosophy: "We have an obligation to the investing public to give that entire public a fair shot at pertinent information that could influence investment decisions." In order to avoid the hazards of "guiding" selected analysts or investors, the company chose to let everyone have the same information on which to base a decision at the same time. What they chose to do with the information was left up to them. Only about 5 percent of those polled responded to the query "What would you like to know about Winnebago and/or the RV industry?" But those that did respond were positive in their reactions. Here are a few comments:

Offhand, I would say that what you are trying to do can only help you and the industry. The better informed the analysts and the public, the more honest an appraisal can be made.

I applaud Winnebago's efforts to improve its disclosure by providing more detailed and frequent reports to the financial community.

Good luck in your endeavor and thanks for being candid with us.

Your desire to provide analysts with the information they need to do their job better is a commendable goal. This will put everyone on an equal footing, will help the financial community to develop a better understanding, and still leave the job of estimating earnings and future prospects to the individual analyst.

We support your proposed policy which would make Winnebago an "equal opportunity company" as far as investor information is concerned.

While analysts of course would like a company to bare its corporate soul and to tell all, that is not yet in the cards. Even a management interested in full and fair disclosure is still reluctant to give aid and comfort to a competitor who is not required to disclose similar information.

At least initially, Winnebago is providing on a monthly basis specific production numbers for its major product line, motor homes, with a breakout between the two types that the company produces. This information is sent to a major financial mailing list and all shareholders, as well as to selected news media, in a one-page "Monthly Report to Shareholders" that also provides management with a more frequent opportunity to communicate with shareholders than is afforded by the quarterly report. It also gives management a prominent forum for disclosing information when appropriate.

Suppose, for example, that analysts are making overly optimistic forecasts of earnings for the quarter or year. The monthly report provides an earlier opportunity than the regular quarterly report to put out appropriate warning signals and perhaps guide all of Wall Street back to a more accurate course without guiding any individuals more accurately than any others.

Earlier I mentioned the fact that about 180 different analysts visited Winnebago between the time of the company's listing in September 1970 and the spring of 1973. That figures out to an average of approximately 1.3 analysts per week during that period of some 138 weeks. Obviously, it was impractical in some weeks for Winnebago to have any analysts at all visit the company (and there were quite a number of weeks when Winnebago was not the apple of Wall Street's eye). Consequently, when the company was able to see visiting analysts, the number actually showing up in Forest City was significant. Indeed, by early spring of 1972, the pressure on Winnebago from the investment community had become considerable.

The company had just completed its first calendar year on the New York Stock Exchange and, as mentioned earlier, in that year had been the leading gainer. As a result, an incredible number of analysts were "discovering" Winnebago Industries, and management was hard-pressed to keep them all supplied with the information they sought.

That spring the pressure became so great that a number of weeks passed in which the company hosted at least one analyst every day of the working week. Since management's primary function is to manage the company, something obviously had to give. Rather than continuing to allow each eager analyst to choose his own day and to determine how much time he would spend seeing the company's facilities, being backgrounded in the investor relations department, and querying, probing, and assessing management at length, the company determined that it would have to establish new ground rules.

A decision was made to entertain visits from the financial community one day a week. No longer would each analyst have his own private seance with management; all who chose to visit the company on the weekly analyst day would receive orientation in the investor relations department, get a plant tour, and spend an hour with the company president and an equal time with the financial vice president.

Within a few weeks, it became obvious that taking care of all the analysts who cared to show up on a given Wednesday was also becoming burdensome, so the number of analysts who could be handled on a daily basis was restricted to four. This was done in their own best interests, since it allowed each to ask his full list of questions and to receive the attention that he or she merited. It wasn't long before some analysts were making appointments six or seven weeks in advance.

Just as the earlier flood of analysts had been an increasing problem for Winnebago management, the status quo in late 1972 had become a problem for the investment community as well. However, since it had become obvious that it was impractical for each individual analyst to have the amount of time with company management that he wanted, even on a weekly basis, Winnebago decided to initiate a new communications device, a practice that was new to the company and relatively rare in industry.

In late January 1973, the company issued the following invitation to the investment community:

> On February 21, 1973, Winnebago Industries will hold the first of what is planned to be a series of open forums for the investment community. To be held at corporate headquarters in Forest City, the meeting will begin at 2:00 P.M., and will present you with the opportunity to meet with a panel of Winnebago management.
>
> These forums, probably to be held on a monthly basis, will replace the smaller, weekly meetings management has held with analysts in the past.
>
> In order for us to properly plan for this first meeting, we need to know if you are planning to attend. Also, there will be no formal presentation. Instead, we encourage your questions. It would help us if you would let us know what sort of questions you'll be asking. That way, we can be better prepared to answer them.

Because a large number of persons are expected to attend the meeting, it will not be possible for management to meet individually with any of those attending.

For those who have never visited Winnebago, or who haven't been to Forest City for some time, there will be plant tours available the morning of February 21.

Although management does not see analysts at Winnebago in between these monthly forums, the company continues to encourage them to come to Forest City for plant tours and for backgrounding by the investor relations department.

It is the philosophy of Winnebago management and its investor relations department that no investor relations program can be cast in concrete. Instead, it must be flexible and able to shift to meet changing circumstances. The only part of the program that does not change is a firm intent to provide full and fair disclosure of information to all elements of the investing public that have an interest in Winnebago, and to provide that information to everyone at the same time. It may be mere naiveté or just a lack of sophistication, but the company believes in the philosophy that all investors are entitled to start the horse race together, armed with the same information. They won't all reach the same conclusion or make the same investment decision, but that is what makes horse racing—and investing—so exciting.

Any investor relations program worth its salt is going to do a good job of communicating, since communications is the name of the game. Depending on whom you are trying to reach and what it is you are trying to say, you will find different ways to achieve that communication. But as in any case of form following function, the best communication will be presented in the simplest form, come quickly to the point it is trying to make, and give the reader or listener the information he seeks in a form that he will understand.

Accuracy, candor, and integrity are the three legs of the tripod on which any solid investor relations program must be based.

Appendix

Introduction

Richard M. Brodrick

YOUR JOB is to represent your company to the investment community and you want to proceed as ethically and professionally as you can. What guidelines do you follow?

You are with your president, who is in discussion with a small group of analysts. Suddenly he blurts out a fact that clearly is material information and that has not yet been made public. What are your responsibilities?

You're writing your first annual report and you want to know the kind of information it *must* contain as opposed to what it *ought to* contain. Where can you go for help?

There probably will never be a book published entitled *Everything You Wanted to Know About Investor Relations but Were Afraid to Ask,* since, unfortunately, all the answers are not readily available. The field is relatively new, and one that is still developing, changing. This is good and

---

Richard M. Brodrick is Director, Corporate Communications, Whittaker Corporation, Los Angeles, Calif.

bad. *Good* because someone just entering the field can, within a reasonable time, familiarize himself with the basic laws and regulations under which he must work. *Bad* because there are still some gray areas that require clarification. This will be forthcoming in good time, but during the interval, it will not be surprising to find some unsuspecting practitioners facing charges as a result of their inadvertent violations of the law.

Investor relations can be cut many ways, segmented, inspected, analyzed, and explained in terms to meet the needs of the diverse functions it involves—financial, legal, communications, analytical. One of the problems in developing a definition that is completely acceptable to everyone —and this includes practitioners within the field itself—is that investor relations is still an emerging profession. It is an unfortunate fact that a host of "experts" find it to their advantage to create a certain mystique about any new area, partly, I suppose, to ensnare potential clients or managements into believing that what has evolved is more an art than a business.

The interesting thing, however, is that investor relations is really only one side of a coin, and the coin itself is somewhat like an electrical conduit. The other side is the financial analyst. Each is trying to transmit, to the very best of his ability, the information from the company (source of power or information) to the entire investment community (end user).

The development of the analytical side actually preceded investor relations, although the latter certainly existed in some undefined form and was not formally centralized. As Wall Street realized that there existed in America a large, untapped market for corporate securities, its sales efforts increased, and with this, the need for better research became acute. Potential securities buyers were demanding more from their brokers than simple execution of orders.

The field was becoming more organized and professional. But while the analytical side of the conduit grew in the absorption and transmission of energy, the other side was developing a blockage, which, if not cleared, would make the conduit virtually worthless. The plain fact was that operating management simply didn't have the time to meet the demands of the analysts who were, quite legitimately, asking more penetrating and knowledgeable questions and in greater volume than ever before.

The only way management had to meet the problem head-on was to centralize this very special communication function in one person (or department) and to charge him with the responsibility of providing the investment community with the information it needed to make sound, informed investment decisions. Thus grew investor relations. But what appeared as a logical solution prompted some problems. On the analytical side it was the reluctance of professional investment analysts to ask for information through intermediaries when formerly they had dealt directly with operating people responsible for the decision making. There was some suspicion on their part that, besides receiving the information they asked for, they were being subjected to a party line. On the other side, the company side, those who found themselves in the investor relations slot realized that they were dealing with a sophisticated audience, not unfriendly, but highly critical of incorrect information or any attempt to con them or the investing public.

Fortunately, both sides developed a respect for each other as it was earned, and both learned to work together despite special difficulties faced by each in his own profession. On the business side, it was the constant effort of the investor relations practitioner to apprise management of the needs of his audience and to educate management on the financial community's reaction to its decisions. This task often became monumental when undertaken against the backdrop of the stock market, which no one has ever accused of being entirely rational and which often did not reflect the full value of the company in the price of its stock. But progress has been made, and management is without question more sensitive now to investment interpretation of its actions than at any time in history. Witness, for example, the number of mergers or acquisitions that have been called off as a result of disappointing stock reaction to the news.

Another problem for the investor relations specialist was the difficulty he encountered in obtaining the information necessary to do his job effectively. The reasons were many: getting others to take the time to develop such information, knowing where to go to get it, winning the trust of those who were able to provide the facts but were simply not used to dispensing it to another (albeit a company man) who spent 50 percent of his working hours talking to outsiders. Unless these hurdles were overcome, which in many instances meant that top management's confidence had to be won over, the investor relations practitioner would be of little value to either his company or the community he was trying to serve.

An additional problem was the increased requirement to transmit more and more information, with a concurrent reduction in the number of channels available to do so. Newspapers have traditionally been the main source of news for the average investor, and with the attrition of this medium, those papers strong enough to stay in business were finding space in their financial sections in tremendous demand. They were able to cover only a portion of the news available to them. (New York City has four fewer major newspapers today than it had ten years ago. Three of them—the *Herald-Tribune,* the *World Telegram & Sun,* and the *Journal-American*—provided extensive financial coverage.) Other media, namely radio and television, simply weren't geared to the needs of the market. Magazines were suited for more in-depth coverage but lacked an essential ingredient—timeliness. This meant the job of communicating became even more difficult while the requirements to communicate became more stringent.

The analyst was having his problems too. First of all, the number of companies to be followed was increasing, thus reducing the time available for any particular area. Industries were also changing, and as companies diversified they became more difficult to analyze and evaluate. The result was that some were relegated to the "not covered" list, a problem which Wall Street still faces and which must be overcome if investors are to have full interpretation of corporate developments.

Reaching the securities salesmen also presented a challenge. We sometimes tend to oversimplify the job an analyst has of communicating with his own audience. He must travel a certain portion of his working hours to meet management on a firsthand basis and evaluate their abilities. He must apportion some of his time for field work if he is to develop a grasp of what his industries are all about. He undoubtedly gets sidetracked on special projects within his firm in the corporate finance area. And he spends a fair amount of time plowing through volumes of news releases, mostly on subjects that are of only marginal interest to him. His primary communications may consist of fast responses to wire inquiries from a sales force representing a wide range of interests and capabilities.

But what difference does this make to the investor relations specialist? Why should he care about the problems of the analyst? Couldn't he ignore them—if they really exist—and proceed through the other channels available to him? The answer is no. The analyst is still the basic link with the investment community. A vital link, and one that cannot be ignored. If the analyst's efficiency in job performance suffers, so does that of the investor relations specialist.

What is so interesting to us in the business is that both the analyst and the investor relations practitioner are living in a fast-changing environment, and neither one can predict with any degree of accuracy what the ground rules will be five or ten years hence. And let's be perfectly honest: they aren't the same now as they were twenty, fifteen, or even ten years ago.

Until the advent of real public ownership, until the time when the Aunt Janes and the Uncle Johns really got into the market, investing was more or less the privilege of a rather select group. Actually, this was the way Wall Street preferred it. Not everyone was capable of investing. One had to be reasonably knowledgeable, affluent, and familiar with the process of the market before he could take the plunge. Not until a few pioneer brokerage firms, and eventually the mighty New York Stock Exchange, got religion did America enter the great arena of the securities market and develop new rules of investing.

But the growth of share ownership and the expansion of the market brought with it some very definite growing pains. No longer could the serious business of investing be treated as a private club for the privileged few. If the league was going to be expanded, the gentlemen's game had to be modified so that everybody was playing by the same rule book.

Wall Street was dealing not with a knowledgeable group but one which, at best, was learning the ropes. Security investment, which had been treated with a certain amount of awe and even distrust, was suddenly being embraced throughout all the ranks of America. Thus began the great love affair between Wall Street and Main Street.

This posed very real problems for everyone concerned with investing, on the corporate side as well as the analytical side, because here was a brand-new element in the equation—the neophyte investor. I'm not so sure that everybody realized the implications of this at the time. It seemed to be a phenomenon we all took for granted. Indeed, it did seem to be a very logical sequence of events, which everyone agreed was a healthy one. And, in fact, it was.

What could be more logical than to have everybody— really everybody—share in America's unlimited growth?

If people's capitalism didn't make sense, then what in fact was private enterprise, our free economic system, all about? Certainly the federal government encouraged share ownership. Certainly most retail-oriented brokerage firms did. And, certainly, the New York Stock Exchange did. What then could possibly hinder the acceptance and successful growth of American capitalism? Nothing, really, if we view the outlook with the perspective of the 1950s.

It is only by hindsight that we realize there have been some roadblocks; and only with the benefit of this hindsight do we see that the road ahead may not be entirely smooth. Witness some of the problems as manifested in

SEC "put-downs" of what it considered unfair practice. Or review some of the more visible conflicts that have been uncovered. It's apparent that there have been some misunderstandings as to what the ground rules are. And mind you, mistakes (if we can use that term) have been made by some very large, respectable organizations on both the Wall Street side and the corporate side. If these organizations and the people associated with them are vulnerable to goofs, what chance, then, does a new investor relations specialist have?

Fortunately, a good one. For in spite of all the monumental toe stubbing, in spite of the volume of words that have been written on the lack of clear-cut guidelines, there does exist a body of knowledge that can be tapped to help him if he is sincerely interested in performing his job to the best of his ability. To say it boils down to common sense would be true only in part. Somehow the investor relations practitioner must get to the information he needs or be guided by an adviser in whom he can trust if he is to be an effective communicator for his company in a very sensitive industry.

And that, in essence, is what the next section is all about: how you get the information you need.

As a representative of your company in the investment community—or the prime link with it—you are expected to be well informed on your company's operation and to have the full confidence of your management. But this is not enough. You must also operate at the highest ethical level, which means being knowledgeable in the regulations that affect your code of conduct. What follows in this section is a concise summary of information for acquainting the serious practitioner with the basic rules and laws relating to investor relations.

Accompanying these laws, which form the foundation blocks in rules of conduct, are the court decisions having a material bearing on investor relations. These should be read most carefully, since they clearly illustrate the trend of government thinking in judging fair practice vis-à-vis the investor. Supporting these interpretations are guides to companies listed on various security exchanges. These should be second nature to any practitioner.

Obviously, there will be situations when not enough time is available for a thorough assimilation of all the reference material and when expert advice will be an immediate need. The question then is where to get help, and how to make certain you are obtaining the best possible counseling available. These are important decisions; and judging by the mis-steps of some advisers, the value of outside financial relations counsel is questionable if not backed by solid knowledge and the highest of ethical standards. Location and size are not as important as a thorough professional attitude.

In other words, if you want to know how to go about it, this is an important section for you. All of the information that follows has been arranged and edited by experts who have spent most of their business careers in the field of investor relations. You should find their commentary valuable and their interpretations of the past twenty years particularly enlightening.

There is no magic to investor relations; but there is hard work, frustration, and thorough enjoyment of an area that is vital to a company's success and which, during the last two decades, has overshadowed virtually every other corporate relations activity.

Essential Laws Relating to
Investor Relations Practices

William H. Dinsmore

FEDERAL

Securities Act of 1933

Concerned primarily with the initial distribution of securities rather than subsequent trading.

Securities Exchange Act of 1934

Concerned with postdistribution trading of securities; provides disclosure requirements for listed and some over-the-counter securities; regulates the activities of the exchange and broker–dealers.

Public Utility Holding Company Act of 1935

Requires all holding companies whose subsidiaries are engaged in electric utility business or retail distribution of gas to register with the SEC.

Trust Indenture Act of 1939

Requires every bond or other debt security offered to the public by the mail or other channels of interstate commerce to be issued under an indenture that has been qualified by the SEC.

Investment Company Act of 1940

Regulates the practices and disclosure requirements of investment companies engaged primarily in the business of investing and reinvesting in securities of other companies.

Investment Advisers Act of 1940

Requires registration with the SEC of persons engaged for compensation in rendering advice or issuing analyses or reports on securities; prohibits fraudulent or deceptive practices by advisers.

Securities Acts Amendments of 1964

Concerned primarily with the extension of disclosure and other requirements for listed stocks to over-the-counter securities.

STATE

Nearly every state has its own securities commission, and federal legislation specifically preserves state controls where applicable. In addition, many states have adopted the Uniform Securities Act of 1956.

The antifraud laws of some states prohibit dissemination of false or misleading corporate publicity. New York State's Martin Act, adopted in 1955, is both broad in scope and specific in defining illegal practices.

Summary of Court Decisions
Affecting Investor Relations

William H. Dinsmore

SEC v. *Arvida*

Arvida is the landmark case in which the SEC sought to establish that publicity amounted to an offer to sell securities in violation of the Section 5 prohibition of such activities prior to or during registration. Such publicity was termed "gun jumping." Originally a private company, Arvida held large tracts of Florida real estate that had belonged to Arthur Vining Davis, one of the founders of Alcoa. When the company went public in 1958, it was of such broad interest that a press conference was held. The district court refused to issue an injunction against two broker–dealers, the company, and individual defendants, but later a permanent injunction was entered by consent.

Cities Service v. *Brophy*

The 1949 case established that an insider may not use corporate information for his own benefit in securities trading. It involved the confidential secretary to the president of Cities Service, who knew that the company was buying its own shares in the open market. Using this information, the secretary would buy before this was to happen and sell afterward.

SEC v. *Cady, Roberts & Co.*

See the chapter "Investor Relations and the Law."

SEC v. *Capital Gains Research Bureau, Inc.*

In 1962 the SEC charged this investment adviser with violating the 1940 Investment Advisers Act when he failed to disclose to clients that he was purchasing for his own account securities which he was also recommending to others for purchase. The case involved a practice known as "scalping," in which an adviser sells his own account out at a profit in the event of a price rise following his recommendation.

Chasins v. *Smith, Barney & Co.*

A radio announcer sued his broker to recover losses in his investments because the broker had failed to reveal that he was a "market maker" in the securities the plaintiff had purchased. The district court agreed the case was actionable under Rule 10b-5.

Chris Craft Industries Inc. v. *Bangor Punta Corp.*

In 1969 the U.S. Second Circuit Court found that a Bangor Punta preregistration press release violated Section 5(c) of the 1933 Act. The press release stated that Bangor Punta would make an exchange offer for Piper Aircraft shares for a package of Bangor Punta securities to be valued at not less than $80 per Piper share.

Crane Co. v. *Westinghouse Air Brake Co.*

In litigation arising from Crane Company's struggle to prevent Westinghouse Air Brake Co. from merging into American Standard Inc., the Second Circuit Court held in

1969 that American Standard was an insider and that its knowledge of its own purchases and sales of Air Brake stock was inside information.

Dolgow v. *Anderson* (Monsanto)

See the chapter "Investor Relations and the Law."

Escott v. *BarChris Construction Corp.*

This case, decided in the U.S. District Court (SDNY) in 1968, imposed strict standards of due diligence upon outside directors, underwriters, and accountants with regard to false registration statements. When BarChris went bankrupt in 1962, attorneys for debenture holders found that the registration statement substantially overstated the backlog for orders and recent gross profits. The plaintiffs did not have to prove that the defendants intentionally deceived anyone, because the defendants had not made a reasonable effort to check the facts.

Gerstle v. *Gamble-Skogmo*

In an amicus brief, the SEC reversed its historic policy that proxy materials should not include any statements about the market value of assets, although it was known the true value considerably exceeded book value. The defendant, Gamble-Skogmo, was trying to bring about a merger with General Outdoor Advertising. The SEC argued, and the Eastern District Court of New York agreed, that "when a proxy statement containing financial statements is attacked as creating a false and misleading inference, it may be no defense that proper accounting procedure has been followed with respect to the financial statements."

SEC v. *Glen Alden*

The SEC charged in 1968 that Glen Alden held private sessions with two mutual funds and an institutionally oriented broker, giving them company divisional sales, earnings and cash flow projections for 1968–72, acquisition plans, and other material, nonpublic information. While denying that any securities had been sold or bought based on the information, Glen Alden consented to an injunction. A long-pending registration statement was cleared the next day.

SEC v. *Great American Industries, Inc.*

The Second Circuit Court held in 1968 that 8-K reports and press releases were materially deficient in failing to disclose finders' fees paid in connection with the purchase of mining properties. The court said that "reasonable traders in stock of a company buying mining property would be influenced by the knowledge that the vendors were willing to pay two-thirds of the price to persons who could produce a buyer."

SEC v. *Investors Management Co., Inc. et al.*

See the chapter "Investor Relations and the Law."

SEC v. *Merrill Lynch*

See the chapter "Investor Relations and the Law."

SEC v. *Pig 'N Whistle Corp.*

The SEC charged a financial public relations firm with helping to prepare and distribute materially false and misleading press releases about Pig 'N Whistle in connection with the offers and sales of securities. Involved, among other things, were the cost and value of certain acquisitions, the company's financial position, the terms and conditions of an acquisition, and the issuance of a finder's fee in connection with another acquisition. Without admitting the allegations, the public relations firm consented to an injunction against future misrepresentations or omissions and agreed to establish procedures for screening future clients and their oral and written public statements.

SEC v. *Texas Gulf Sulphur*

See the chapter "Investor Relations and the Law." In addition to its importance in setting new standards for the omission or inclusion of material facts in a press release, the *Texas Gulf* case established new concepts broadening the definition of "insiders," when they may buy or sell their company's securities, the acceptance of stock options, and liability for "tipping" material information to others.

Policies and Guidelines of the Major Stock Exchanges

Arthur R. Roalman

KNOWN STOCK EXCHANGES throughout the world were asked to send information for this section. As might be expected, the New York Stock Exchange provided the most meaningful information. The American Stock Exchange had surprisingly little to offer on the subject. From the several dozen pieces of information received, it is obvious that the fundamental document that anyone concerned with investor relations should be familiar with is a manual published by the New York Stock Exchange, Inc. (11 Wall St., New York, N.Y. 10005). Entitled *Expanded Policy on Timely Disclosures,* this valuable source of information forms the base, philosophical and mechanical, for most investor relations efforts.

The following excerpts from that manual are published with permission of the New York Stock Exchange. They reflect the information that is provided in the manual, but are presented as they are here to help readability.

Handling Information to Be Released

1. "A corporation whose stock is listed . . . is expected to release quickly to the public any news or information which might reasonably be expected to materially affect the market for securities. . . .

2. "A corporation should also act promptly to dispel unfounded rumors which result in unusual market activity or price variations.

3. "[In situations involving] negotiations leading to acquisitions and mergers, stock splits, the making of arrangements preparatory to an exchange or tender offer changes in dividend rates or earnings, calls for redemption, new contracts, products, or discoveries, . . . [if] unusual market activities should arise, the company should be prepared to make an immediate public announcement.

4. ". . . fairness requires that the company make an immediate public announcement as soon as confidential disclosures . . . are made to 'outsiders.'

5. "As a minimum, they [the disclosures] should include those disclosures made to 'outsiders.'

6. "Where an initial announcement cannot be specific or complete, it will need to be supplemented from time to time as more definitive or different terms are discussed or determined.

7. "Corporate employees, as well as directors and officers, should be regularly reminded as a matter of policy that they must not disclose confidential information they may receive in the course of their duties and must not attempt to take advantage of such information themselves.

    •   •   •   •   •   •

10. "If during the course of a discussion with analysts substantive material not previously published is disclosed,

that material should be simultaneously released to the public.

11. "On the other hand, it is entirely appropriate for company officials to discuss such matters as the trend of business with the specialist, much as they would with bankers, stockholders, security analysts, or anyone having a legitimate interest in the company.

12. "Any director of a corporation who is a partner, officer, or employee of a member organization should recognize that his first responsibility in this area is to the corporation on whose Board he serves. Thus, a member firm director must meticulously avoid any disclosure of inside information to his partners, employees of the firm, his customers, or his research or trading departments.

13. "Where a representative of a member organization is not a director but is acting in an advisory capacity to a company and discussing confidential matters, the ground rules should be substantially the same as those that apply to a director."

Procedure for Public Release of Information

1. "The normal method of publication of important corporate data is by means of a press release. This may be either by telephone or in written form. Any release of information that could reasonably be expected to have an impact on the market for a company's securities should be given to the wire services and the press FOR IMMEDIATE RELEASE. Clearly, a corporation cannot properly assume responsibility for the security of such important information in the hands of persons or organizations beyond its control.

2. "The spirit of the IMMEDIATE RELEASE policy is not considered to be violated on weekends where a 'hold for Sunday or Monday A.M.'s' is used to obtain a broad public release of the news. This procedure facilitates the combination of a press release with a mailing to shareholders.

3. "Annual and quarterly earnings, dividend announcements, acquisitions, mergers, tender offers, stock splits, and major management changes are examples of news items that should be handled on an immediate release basis. News of major new products, contract awards, expansion plans, and discoveries very often fall into the same category. Unfavorable news should be reported as promptly and candidly as the favorable. Reluctance or unwillingness to release a negative story or an attempt to disguise unfavorable news endangers a management's reputation for integrity. Changes in accounting methods to mask such occurrences can have a similar long-term impact.

4. "It should be a corporation's primary concern to assure that news will be handled in proper perspective. This necessitates appropriate restraint, good judgment, and careful adherence to the facts. Any projections of financial data, for instance, should be soundly based, appropriately qualified, conservative, and factual. Excessive or misleading conservatism should be avoided. Likewise, the repetitive release of essentially the same information is not appropriate.

5. "Few things are more damaging to a corporation's stockholder relations or to the general public's regard for corporate securities than information improperly withheld whether inadvertently or willfully. On the other hand, a mere deluge of press releases is not to be used since important items can become confused with trivia.

6. "Premature announcements of new products whose

commercial application cannot yet be realistically evaluated should be avoided. So should overly optimistic forecasts, exaggerated claims, and unwarranted promises. And should subsequent developments indicate that performance will not match earlier projections, this too should be reported and explained.

7. "Judgment must be exercised as to the timing of a public release on those corporate developments where the immediate release policy is not involved or where disclosure would endanger the company's goals or provide information helpful to a competitor. In these cases, it is helpful to weigh the fairness to both present and potential stockholders who at any given moment may be considering buying or selling the company's stock.

8. "The market action of a company's securities should be closely watched at a time when consideration is being given to significant corporate matters. If rumors or unusual market activity indicate that information on impending developments has leaked out, a frank and explicit announcement is clearly required. If rumors are in fact false or inaccurate, they should be promptly denied or clarified. If they are correct, however, an immediate, candid statement to the public as to the state of negotiations or the state of development of corporate plans in the rumored area must be made directly and openly. Such statements are essential despite the business inconvenience which may be caused and even though the matter may not as yet have been presented to the company's Board of Directors for consideration.

9. "News which ought to be the subject of immediate publicity must be released by the fastest available means. The 'fastest available means' may vary in individual cases and according to the time of day. Ordinarily, this requires

a release to the public press by telephone, telegraph, or hand delivery, or some combination thereof. Transmittal of such a release to the press solely by mail is not considered satisfactory. Similarly, release of such news exclusively to the local press outside of New York City would not be sufficient for adequate and prompt disclosure to the investing public.

10. "To insure adequate coverage, releases requiring immediate publicity should be given to Dow Jones & Company, Inc., to Reuters Economic Services, and to Associated Press and United Press International. These releases should also be given to one or more of the newspapers of general circulation in New York City which regularly publish financial news.

11. "Two copies of each such press release should be sent promptly to the Exchange, to the attention of the Department of Stock List.

12. "It is suggested that every news release include the name and telephone number of a company official who will be available if a newspaper or news wire service desires to confirm or clarify the release with the company."

Although the current listing agreement proposed by the New York Stock Exchange is not included here, anyone concerned with investor relations, whether his firm is listed on the New York Stock Exchange or not, should write to the Exchange and get a copy of the agreement, which forms a strong conceptual base for almost any investor relations effort.

Other exchanges have different reporting requirements. For example, the Boston Stock Exchange specifies that "corporate reports must be sent to stockholders annually and semi-annually, with quarterly reports published in major newspapers and financial publications." The Boston Exchange doesn't require quarterly reports to shareholders. But the other exchanges do observe concepts of timely disclosure in internal handling of confidential corporate matters on the same basis as the New York Stock Exchange. Here's a paragraph worth noting from the Boston Exchange:

> Security analysts play an increasingly important role in the evaluation and interpretation of the financial affairs of listed companies. Annual reports, quarterly reports, and interim releases cannot by their nature provide all of the financial and statistical data that should be available to the investing public. The Exchange recommends that corporations observe an "open door" policy in their relations with security analysts, financial writers, shareowners, and others who have a legitimate investment interest in the company's affairs. A company should not give information to one inquirer which it would not give to another. Nor should it reveal information it would not willingly give to the press for publication. Thus, for corporations to give advance earnings, dividend, stock split, merger, or tender information to analysts, whether representing an institution, brokerage house, investment advisor, large stockholder, or anyone else, would be clearly incompatible with Exchange policy. On the other hand, it should not withhold information in which analysts or other members of the investing public have a warrantable interest.

The following statement, from a speech given by Huntly W. F. McKay, vice president for market development and research at the Toronto Stock Exchange, bears heavily on the subject of corporate investor relations.

"First, let me deal with the matter of corporate disclosure. It is the view of the Toronto Stock Exchange that in those situations where corporations seek capital from the public, such corporations have a responsibility to insure that the public is kept fully informed regarding developments that relate to the corporation, particularly those developments which may affect the value of the equities of the corporation.

"The Toronto Stock Exchange has now a fairly complex set of regulations which all listed companies must comply with in order to list on the Exchange, and in order to maintain such a listing on the Exchange.

"The requirement that all listed companies issue annual reports within six months of the end of their fiscal year has been a requirement on the Exchange for some years. More recently, however, the Toronto Stock Exchange has decided that shareholders require a more current financial picture of listed companies. Accordingly, as of January 1 of this year [1969] the Toronto Exchange instituted a policy that all listed companies, except a small number that have been able to convince the Exchange that they deserve to be exempted, must issue quarterly statements. In effect, shareholders and the investing public are provided with four financial reports during each fiscal year from each listed company.

"One of the reasons which the Exchange believes is sound in respect to requiring listed companies to provide more information has to do with the fact that many of the large financial institutions in Canada have repeatedly stated that among the various reasons they channel large portions of their investment funds into the American market is the fact that the listed companies in that market issue quarterly statements. The financial institutions, because of their fiduciary responsibility to their clients, feel that it is essential to have a current picture of the financial position of the company or companies in which they are investing sizable sums of money. And, of course, this point of view is quite sound. Consequently, the Toronto Stock Exchange concluded that one way in which to inspire a greater confidence by the financial institutions, and other investors who argue that there is inadequate financial information regarding listed companies in Canada, was to insure the existence of current financial information. Obviously, whether you are a large financial institution or a private individual, it is much more reassuring to be able to look at a financial report of a company, in which you are considering placing a sum of money, which is no older than two or three months, for example. With such information, it is possible to make more rational and sound decisions in respect to the investing of your money.

"The Toronto Stock Exchange has also recognized that there are limitations in respect to annual reports and quarterly statements. In effect, it is recognized that certain events can occur which will materially affect the value of the shares of a listed company, and that these events are of such significance that it is improper to wait until the quarterly statement is issued before informing shareholders and the potential investing public about such developments.

"Consequently, the Toronto Stock Exchange has adopted, and enforces, a policy known as the 'Timely Disclosure Policy.' This policy imposes upon the listed companies a requirement that where there are significant developments within the company, the company must as quickly as possible make an announcement regarding these developments. Such an announcement avoids insider trading and insures that investors and potential investors are able to make decisions based on current and official information.

"To insure that the Exchange's Timely Disclosure Policy is followed by the listed companies, the Toronto Stock Exchange's Market Surveillance Department is constantly contacting listed companies by telephone, to inquire if, in view of the lively market action of their stock, the executives of these companies know of any reason the stock of their company has shown an unusual upward or downward movement. If the company acknowledges that there are developments, the Exchange insists that as soon as it is practicable, the company make an announcement regarding its operations. Some instances where the information is sufficiently significant, the Exchange stops the trading in the shares of the company until the company has been able to make an announcement."

It would be impossible to print here the speech about insider trading that was given by J. R. Kimber, president of the Toronto Stock Exchange, but you might find it worthwhile to write to him and ask for copies. It's entitled "A Second Look at Insider Trading."

Although the foregoing excerpts constitute the bulk of the investor relations information offered by the major exchanges to corporations, there are other printed materials available from the exchanges with which investor relations people might want to be familiar. Among them are the following from the New York Stock Exchange:

The Exchange. This monthly magazine describes, in popular readable form, reports on investing, industries, and related matters.

The Language of Investing, which is intended to make the stock market less mysterious.

Investors' Notebook, a series of booklets that are further identified as "A Guide to the Working Language of Wall Street." They also are designed to make the New York Stock Exchange less mysterious.

Understanding Financial Statements, which tries to help the investor understand those sometimes mystifying documents.

Margin, a recent booklet that describes margin buying of securities.

Understanding Bonds and Preferred Stocks, a reading guide for the individual investor.

Sources of Aid for the
Investor Relations Professional

Quentin J. Hietpas

"WHY ARE SO many managements so stupid when it comes to dealing with us?" complained a frustrated securities analyst recently as she recounted her experiences with one company after another. Then, as an afterthought, she added, "Probably because they don't want to listen to advice."

This paper will explore two sources available to investor relations officers to help them do their jobs better. The first part will deal with the use of outside investor relations consultants and include some comments on one of the highly specialized areas in the field, the proxy solicitor. The second part will describe various periodicals and reference works that constitute the tools of the business.

THE OUTSIDE CONSULTANT

A familiar question facing the management of a company that is about to institute an investor relations program is:

Quentin J. Hietpas is Vice President, Communications, DATA 100 Corporation, Minneapolis, Minn.

Should we set up an in-house capability, or should we go outside and hire a consultant?

The decision will ultimately rest not only on economic considerations but also on the caliber of the people available. Experienced and capable investor relations people are hard to find. They are truly at a premium. Therefore, it is important to determine at the outset exactly what it is you are buying: Are you seeking only counseling to help you diagnose problems and recommend solutions? Are you seeking services to help you execute your programs? Or are you seeking a combination of the two?

If you can afford it, the practical answer is an inside investor relations specialist who works with an outside agency to provide consultation on a continuing basis and services when they are needed.

In fact, many small- and medium-size companies employ consultants to do the whole job—counseling and servicing. This occurs when no inside staff exists, or where it is very small. In this case, the consultant works with the client on an almost daily basis. In effect, he becomes the investor relations staff of that company.

Why go outside at all? What do investor relations counselors bring to the ball game? Actually, many capabilities, if they are used correctly. There are three that are especially important.

Perhaps the greatest dimension that the counselor brings is *impartial perspective*. The old adage about the forest and the trees applies here in spades. Management feels it lacks the internal expertise to determine what is needed, and usually its prime motivation for going outside is to find a fresh viewpoint. Consultants can conduct an impartial audit of present activities. They can help develop an internal investor relations program. They can utilize broad expertise from many sources to zero in on a management problem. And, importantly, their outside status gives them a unique freedom to ask pointed questions and provide impartial feedback from the financial community.

The second reason why companies go outside is for the sake of *utility*. It's faster. They can get a professional job under way more quickly than if they developed an in-house capability.

The third reason is *cost*. Outside counsel is frequently more economical, particularly when a wide range of services, and perhaps geographic coverage, is needed only on a periodic basis. Outside counsel can help to smooth out the peaks and valleys, which are typical of the investor relations workload, without the company's having to add additional inside staff. Outside standby services will certainly cost money, but it is frequently far less than what an overstaffed department would cost. The outside consultant can add specialties "when needed," which would be far more expensive if they were maintained on a full-time basis internally.

There are certain things the outside counselor cannot do.

He cannot make a company what it is not. This is particularly true in investor relations where management is subject to the searching scrutiny of securities analysts and the probing questions of financial journalists who are trained to look for weaknesses. Jonathan Swift's advice two hundred years ago certainly applies to the investor relations counselor of today: he cannot make a silk purse out of a sow's ear. Objectivity is essential. Even the most subtle shading of the truth can do irreparable harm to the company.

Also, outside counselors cannot speak in place of management. It is true that they can keep the press and the financial community abreast of current developments, and they can answer many basic questions. But ultimately the reporter or the analyst will want to talk directly to management. Management cannot abdicate this responsibility—it cannot pass off the obligation to a convenient "outside" middleman. The analyst and the financial newsman want to speak directly to management. Why? Because management is obviously closer to the basic information. Firsthand contact also gives the analyst an opportunity to evaluate management, which has an important bearing on whether or not he recommends the company.

Outside counsel also cannot read the mind of the management it serves. This means that management must level completely. It cannot withhold certain important facts while revealing only favorable information. Consultants, to be effective in their counseling capacity, must be looked upon as a part of top management. A good outside counsel will demand this for his own protection, because he now is being held legally responsible, along with inside management, for the accuracy and completeness of the information he disseminates.

As smaller companies without an internal staff look toward outside help, they must consider their entire communications needs, including press relations, community relations, and possibly product publicity, as well as specialized investor relations help. Given these needs, they will probably look toward a general public relations firm with some expertise in investor relations. This makes good sense, particularly for the smaller company with a limited budget. Cost would likely prohibit the hiring of individual specialists in each of these areas. But remember, just because a firm is competent in general public relations, it does not necessarily follow that it is competent in investor relations.

Indeed, there are many large corporations that retain large public relations firms with known capability in a number of specialized areas.

A reputable consultant will never guarantee to effect a more favorable price for the stock of his client. He will never point to such strong "connections" in the financial community that brokerage houses will immediately start pushing that particular security. An experienced investor relations consultant will not make these claims. Neither will the reputable public relations generalist.

Instead, their claims will be based on the fact that they have successfully communicated in the past the financial story of their clients to a variety of interested people. That's all. Investor relations experience means a familiarity with the basic rules of the Securities and Exchange Commission and the various stock exchanges. It means a basic understanding of the financial aspects of a company. It means a basic familiarity with communications techniques to satisfy the needs of securities analysts, stockholders, and the financial press.

To make the company–consultant relationship successful, management must clearly define in advance what it wants from its consultant. More than for any other reason, an investor relations program involving outside consultants will fail because the company did not know what it wanted in the first place. So before you start looking for a consultant, decide specifically what you want him to do. Start by clearly defining the corporate goals for investor relations. This will help immeasurably in deciding on an outside counselor. If you have an inside department, draw a distinct line between what the outsider will do and what the insider will do. Be sure to define how they will interrelate.

When you enter the relationship, do so with the idea that it will be a continuing arrangement, as opposed to a project-type one. It is only when both sides work together over a long period that the necessary rapport can be established.

After you have retained a firm of outside consultants, provide them with backing within the organization. Act one way or the other on their recommendations; don't leave them in limbo. Keep in close touch with them. And again, keep them fully informed of both the good and the bad. Only if you follow these four guidelines can the relationship truly work. Remember, to be totally effective the consultant must retain his objectivity. Therefore, if the outsider is good, he'll resist being a "yes man."

HOW THE CONSULTANT WORKS

There's a basic approach to the communications process that all professionals follow to some degree, although each has his modifications. Basically, the outside consultant will engage in an initial period of fact finding—talking to analysts, stockholders, and the financial press in order to appraise the company's problems and potentials. The purpose here is to determine the basic investor relations goals. He will need help from management in this task, including a frank discussion of corporate goals, philosophies, long-range plans, and strengths and weaknesses. Candid, full disclosure at this point is a must.

Next, he'll translate the results of his fact finding into a plan. Its objectives should be oriented to the total objectives of the corporation. A good counselor will never predict miracles. His plan should contain a specific timetable, but if he promises a particular price–earnings ratio by a definite date, watch out. Total success is as rare in an investor relations program as it is in any program. Variables are bound to occur. A realistic investor relations plan will outline the results anticipated, but it will never, never guarantee these results. A good plan will also contain a detailed budget.

At this point, management must make a decision. It's either go or no-go. It is important to remember that management has no obligation to accept the program, either in total or in part. However, the previously determined professional capability of the consultant must be kept in mind if there is to be mutual understanding and confidence during the implementation phase. Once the plan is established and the costs are agreed upon, a written contract, in my mind, is essential. Spell out the conditions so that both parties understand them completely. This will prevent a lot of possible disillusionment in the future.

After the basic fact finding and the planning are complete, next comes the third step—implementation of the communications program. This may be done by the inside staff, the outside counsel, or a combination of both.

The final step in the process is constant evaluation of the program through playback analysis from the financial community.

WHAT TO LOOK FOR IN A CONSULTANT

Whether the outside consultant is employed in strictly a consulting capacity or to actively implement the investor relations program, make sure that his thinking is the same as that of any corporate manager. Outside counsel must be results-oriented. The corporate goals must be his goals. In fact, a good approach is to evaluate the qualifications of an outside consultant just as you would if you were adding another employee to the top management of your organization. What would you look for?

Empathy. Whoever works directly on your account must, obviously, get along with the person supervising that account within the organization, as well as with the chief executive and the chief financial officer of the company. As you are interviewing a prospective consulting agency, ask to visit with the particular person who will be working on your account. In addition to ascertaining his intelligence, integrity, and experience, make sure that the consultant is on the same wavelength as his counterpart inside the company. Make sure that they will enjoy working together. The whole task will be a lot easier.

Courage. Look for the ability on the part of the outsider to stand up for what he or she believes.

Reputation and background. Check out the reputation of the principals of the firm with care. If necessary, employ a professional organization to do this.

Experience. Ask for specific details about programs that the outsider has done for other clients. Investigate carefully the background and experience of each of the staff members who might be working on your account.

Other employers. If it is not offered, ask for the client list of the outside consultant and find out how long these clients have been employing him. Ask to see specific work he has done for them. Ask about turnover. Ask the names of former clients and why the relationship was terminated.

Financial references. Don't forget to check banking, business, and legal sources.

Ethics. Look into this aspect very carefully. As in many

professions, both investor relations specifically and public relations in general have their share of charlatans. The Public Relations Society of America (PRSA) has its code of ethics for investor relations practitioners. Check to see if the outside consultant is a member of PRSA and whether he subscribes to the code. Ask security analysts and financial newsmen about his ethical reputation. Check the Securities and Exchange Commission for possible violations of the securities acts.

Feel free to ask any questions you want. Do not confine yourself to interviewing only one outsider. Talk to at least two. Carefully consider whether a local firm, which knows the local situation and has people readily available to managers, is better than a national firm that obviously has greater geographic capabilities, including direct daily contact with Wall Street. Both have strong pluses—it depends on your particular needs.

HOW CONSULTANTS CHARGE

It is important at the outset of your relationship with your outside consultant to clearly establish guidelines as to how you will pay for services rendered. Don't be bashful about asking to have a clear understanding of costs well in advance. You have every right to expect an accurate, detailed cost estimate for your program, and this can be prepared as soon as there is a meeting of the minds and a plan has been established. Such an estimate would include fixed costs in the form of a previously agreed upon basic fee arrangement, plus estimated variable (out-of-pocket) costs.

There are basically two factors that produce costs: (1) the amount of time required and (2) the number of staff people involved on your account.

Generally, outside consultants charge for their services (fixed costs) in one of three ways: (1) a predetermined monthly retainer fee, which can run from as low as $750 to as high as $5,000, depending upon the extent to which the two cost factors are involved; (2) a predetermined retainer fee, plus a monthly billing for actual staff time on an hourly basis; or (3) a basic monthly retainer fee that entitles the client to a maximum agreed-upon number of hours of staff time, to which are added increments for services beyond that basic fee. Often a consultant may be retained to do a special project on a one-time fee basis.

Of course, in addition to the basic fee, out-of-pocket costs are extra. Generally they are billed at cost. Costs of certain collateral materials, such as artwork, printing, photography, and so forth, are often marked up at the standard rate of about 18 percent, but this practice should be clearly defined in the contract.

HOW TO FIND A CONSULTANT

There are two national professional organizations to which investor relations professionals belong. They are the National Investor Relations Institute (NIRI), 1255 New Hampshire Avenue N.W., Washington, D.C. 20036, and the Public Relations Society of America (PRSA), 845 Third Avenue, New York, N.Y. 10022.

NIRA has a directory listing all its members.

PRSA has a comprehensive directory of members, of which a section is devoted to a listing of counselors. However, not all of these counselors have specialties in investor relations. The PRSA directory also indicates which members have been accredited by the association as having met certain minimum professional and ethical standards.

There is another directory, published by the J. R. O'Dwyer Co. Inc., 271 Madison Avenue, New York, N.Y. 10016, that contains a geographical listing of public relations firms and an index showing which companies employ other public relations firms.

In addition, *Investment Dealers' Digest,* 150 Broadway, New York, N.Y. 10038, publishes a semiannual listing of public relations firms classified according to the corporations they serve. It is titled the *Financial Publicists Directory.*

By cross-checking the four directories, you can arrive at some basic directions for contacting an outside consultant. For example, suppose you were a food company located in Minneapolis and have decided to look for an outside consultant. Checking other food companies in Minneapolis, you would find in the O'Dwyer directory that International Multifoods uses Georgeson & Co., Green Giant uses Padilla & Speer, and General Mills uses R. J. Sullivan (which has an associate, Northstar Public Relations, in Minneapolis). Upon further checking in the *Financial Publicists Directory,* you would find that the Peavey Co. employs Don Braman & Associates. Then you might check the NIRI directory to see if these firms have members in NIRI. Finally, you can check the PRSA directory to further determine if they are listed in the counselors' section and whether they have accredited members in their firms.

Both PRSA and NIRI have local chapters. Local chapters are listed in the PRSA directory along with the officers of each chapter. This also can serve as a starting point in finding local counselors; most local chapters have their own directory.

Additional important sources are analysts who follow

your company, financial newsmen, and your investment banker.

THE OUTSIDE PROXY SOLICITOR

One of the most specialized areas in the investor relations field is proxy solicitation. Proxy solicitors are hired for three main reasons: (1) to assume the responsibility for solicitation of proxies from brokers and nominees so that management's time is not wasted in an area in which it may have little expertise; (2) to insure a large vote of approval when an important corporate proposal is being submitted to stockholders; and (3) to insure that at all times the required number of proxy votes will be obtained.

Many companies have found that it is time-consuming and disruptive to solicit proxies from brokers, nominees, and institutional holders. An outside organization assumes that responsibility for them and sets up the mechanics of the solicitation, delivers the proxy materials to their destination, and follows up with proxy clerks. The outside proxy solicitors know exactly where and how to deliver material and how to best enlist the cooperation of the back-office personnel of brokers and nominees.

The proxy solicitation responsibility in most companies falls to the office of the corporate secretary. In many companies the corporate secretary function is within the legal department, and there is enough to do without saddling that department with the responsibility of obtaining a large vote. In addition, the advantage of having a proxy solicitor is that he does this for a living all year long, whereas the corporate secretary does it only once a year. The outsider therefore is more likely to know the shortcuts.

What do you look for in hiring a proxy solicitor? Probably the most important factor is his reputation for being able to get a difficult job done. Inexperienced solicitors will waste valuable time and will simply not be familiar enough with the techniques to be totally effective.

There are four leading proxy soliciting firms in the field (the first is the largest):

Georgeson & Co., 100 Wall Street, New York, N.Y. 10005

D. F. King & Co., Inc., 20 Exchange Place, New York, N.Y. 10005

The Kissel-Blake Organization, Inc., 50 Broadway, New York, N.Y. 10004

G. R. Squires & Co., Inc., 74 Trinity Place, New York, N.Y. 10006

REFERENCE AIDS

There are a number of periodicals, magazines, newsletters, directories, reports, and services that are indispensable to the investor relations practitioner in the performance of his job. Following are some of the major references in the field, including (1) eight general references that are used almost daily by the investor relations person, (2) four periodicals that are valuable in helping keep track of current trends and thinking in the securities field, (3) four newsletters that can help the investor relations person keep up on the latest thinking in his field, (4) a listing of some of the major investment advisory services, and, finally, (5) a compilation of some of the directories that can help the investor relations officer to better analyze corporate stockholdings.

No attempt has been made to be complete or exhaustive in these listings. In each case there are undoubtedly other excellent references that have been omitted for space reasons.

GENERAL REFERENCES

The Financial Analysts Federation Membership Directory
A yearly publication that lists Federation officers and members, giving firm name, address, and telephone number. Indexed geographically and by specialty. Available from The Financial Analysts Federation, Tower Suite, 219 East 42nd Street, New York, N.Y. 10017

Security Dealers of North America
A directory of over 10,000 securities dealers and brokers in the United States and Canada. Lists name, address, telephone and teletype numbers, date established, general character of the business, and class of securities handled. Available from Standard & Poor's Corporation, 345 Hudson Street, New York, N.Y. 10014.

The E-Z Telephone Directory of Brokers and Banks
Lists all stock brokers and banks in the New York area. An invaluable tool for the investor relations person who frequently calls addresses on Wall Street. Available from The E-Z Telephone Directory Corp., 666 Franklin Avenue, Garden City, N.Y. 11530.

Dun & Bradstreet Million Dollar Directory
Lists companies with a net worth of one million dollars or more. Broken down alphabetically, geographically, by product classification, with pertinent data. Available from Dun & Bradstreet, Inc., 99 Church Street, New York, N.Y. 10007.

Money Market Directory

A directory of 10,000 institutions and their portfolio managers. A practical guide to helping the investor relations person locate key decision makers among the institutions. Available from Money Market Directories, Inc., 52 Park Avenue, New York, N.Y. 10016.

American Stock Exchange Guide

A directory containing the constitution, rules, and policies of the American Stock Exchange. Available from Commerce Clearing House, Inc., 4025 West Peterson Avenue, Chicago, Ill. 60646.

New York Stock Exchange Guide

A directory that contains the constitution and rules of the New York Stock Exchange, along with pertinent SEC requirements. Available from Commerce Clearing House, Inc., 4025 West Peterson Avenue, Chicago, Ill. 60646.

Poor's Register of Corporations, Directors, and Executives

A listing that gives pertinent information on over 200,-000 individual officers and directors of corporations. Available from Standard & Poor's Corporation, 345 Hudson Street, New York, N.Y. 10014.

PERIODICALS

Financial Analysts Journal

Published bimonthly for members of The Financial Analysts Federation, with subscriptions also open to the general public. Excellent analytical, financial, and economic articles. Available from The Financial Analysts Federation, Tower Suite, 219 East 42nd Street, New York, N.Y. 10017.

Institutional Investor

An indispensable publication for the investor relations professional. Published monthly, articles are aimed at professional investment managers and give a good insight into current trends and thinking on Wall Street. Available from Institutional Investor, Circulation Department, 2160 Patterson Street, Cincinnati, Ohio. 45214.

Financial Executive

Published monthly. Contains excellent articles about current trends in finance accounting and controllership. Available to members of the Financial Executives Institute, 633 Third Avenue, New York, N.Y. 10017.

The Wall Street Letter

A chatty, highly readable weekly report to the securities industry and allied fields on current happenings on Wall Street. Available from Institutional Investor Systems, Inc., 140 Cedar Street, New York, N.Y. 10006.

NEWSLETTERS

The Corporate Communications Report

Published bimonthly. Contains in-depth articles on items of direct interest to the investor relations officer. Available from Corpcom Services, Inc., 112 East 31st Street, New York, N.Y. 10006.

Investor Relations Newsletter

Published monthly. Contains news and reports on subjects of direct interest to the investor relations professional. Available from Enterprise Publications, 20 N. Wacker Drive, Chicago, Ill. 60606.

NIRI Notes

Published bimonthly. Contains educational items and news notes. Available to members of the National Investor Relations Institute, 1255 New Hampshire Avenue N.W., Room 1030, Washington, D.C. 20036.

Trends

A monthly newsletter on subjects of interest to management and investor relations professionals. Available from Georgeson & Co., 100 Wall Street, New York, N.Y. 10005.

INVESTMENT ADVISORY SERVICES

Argus Research Reports. Argus is a completely independent research organization that provides continuing analysis and review of about 350 leading stocks.

Argus Weekly Staff Report. Highlights about five stocks weekly for its clients. Available only to clients from Argus Research Corp., 140 Broadway, New York, N.Y. 10005.

Standard & Poor's. This organization has a number of directories, publications, and services. Among them are:

Earnings Forecaster. Report of current earnings estimates of over a thousand companies by Standard & Poor's and other brokerage firms. Includes source of estimate, date of estimate, and, where possible, estimate for the following year, as well as actual earnings for the past year.

Industry Surveys. Economic and investment analysis of forty-four leading industries and a summary of Canadian industries, together with over a thousand of their constituent companies. Subscribers receive an annual basic survey and three to four current surveys, plus monthly trends and projections.

Stock Guide. Statistical and investment advisory book listing financial data for 4,700 issues. Includes investment characteristics of stock, earnings and dividend estimates, and monthly highs and lows for a quick analysis. An invaluable, handy reference booklet that is popular with those associated with the securities industry.

Stock Summary. Provides ticker symbol, S&P ranking, current highs and lows, par value, dividend yield, ex-dividend, date paid, dividend current and previous year, interim and long-term earnings, nature of business, capital, and working capital.

Stock Records. Factual information on American and foreign corporations and their securities. Descriptions and histories of all corporations in which there is investor interest. Includes a Daily Corporate News edition.

Stock Reports. Standard & Poor's well-known, one-page (printed both sides) research reports on listed and over-the-counter companies, written and researched by S&P analysts. The familiar yellow sheets (for NYSE-listed companies), blue sheets (for AMEX-listed companies), and green sheets (for over-the-counter companies) are widely used throughout the securities industry as a quick, ready reference.

Each of the above services is available from Standard & Poor's Corporation, 345 Hudson Street, New York, N.Y. 10014.

Moody's Investors Service. Moody's is another highly respected and widely used investment advisory service.

Moody's Handbook of Common Stocks. This service is designed primarily for individual stock buyers who are looking into the qualifications of individual issues before acting on advice or suggestions. This volume contains reports on over 2,500 common stocks, more than 1,500 in tabular form, and 1,110 arranged alphabetically (with charts and detailed statistics) from which the typical American investor selects the majority of his holdings.

Moody's Industrial News Reports. These reports provide important factual information on company history, management personnel, location of offices and plants, and financial statements, including comparative income, long-term record of earnings, comparative balance sheets, financial and operating data. Available from Moody's Investor Service, Inc., 99 Church Street, New York, N.Y. 10007.

The Value Line Investment Survey. Provides continuing analysis and review of leading stocks in industries and special situations. Each weekly edition covers full-page analyses of about a hundred stocks; each of the stocks is reviewed in revised full-page reports at least four times a year. Available from Arnold Bernhard & Co., Inc., 5 East 44th Street, New York, N.Y. 10017.

The above major investment advisory services deal with the analysis of the fundamentals of securities. In addition, there are a number of "chart services" that map the performance of various securities. Two of them are:

Stock Chart Service. One of Mansfield's chart services. This one publishes over 1,100 stock charts every week plus 600 more every two weeks. Also included every week are pages containing analyses and market averages. Available from R. W. Mansfield Co., 26 Journal Square, Jersey City, N.J. 07306.

Stock Advisory Service. Another well-known chart service. Available from John Magee, Inc., 360 Worthington Street, Springfield, Mass. 01103.

There are scores of other investment advisory services and market letters with high reputations that will take smaller advisory accounts. A listing of these can be found in the monthly magazine *Sources and Ideas,* published by Select Information Exchange, 2095 Broadway, New York, N.Y. 10023.

DIRECTORIES

Nominee List

This handbook is invaluable in learning the identity of shareholders who hold their stock in nominee name. It contains an alphabetical listing of nominees with their employer identification numbers. A second section is arranged by state and by custodian or principal within the state. The final section is an alphabetical list of investment funds and foundations with custodial banks and the nominees that they use. Available from American Society of Corporate Secretaries, Inc., One Rockefeller Plaza, New York, N. Y. 10020.

Vickers Guide to Investment Company Portfolios

This service reports the common stock portfolio holdings of common stocks by mutual funds. The *Vickers Guide to Insurance Company Portfolios—Common Stocks* publishes a companion service. It reports the common stock portfolio holdings of 949 casualty and life insurance companies doing business in the United States and Canada. The common stock portfolios of 105 separate accounts of these companies are also reported upon. Available from Vickers Associates, Inc., 226 New York Avenue, Huntington, N.Y. 11743.

Investment Companies

Basic information on open-end and closed-end funds in the United States and Canada, including portfolio holdings, investment policy, and charts showing record of achievement. This service enables the investor relations officer to ascertain which funds are holding stock in his corporation and the number of shares held. Available from Weisenberger Services, Inc., One New York Plaza, New York, N.Y. 10004.

Facts on the Funds

Analyzes the portfolio activity of the largest mutual funds and closed-end investment companies in America as to shares purchased, shares sold, and shares now held. Available from Weisenberger Services, Inc., One New York Plaza, New York, N.Y. 10004.

Mutual Fund Directory

Lists all open-end funds, regardless of size or type. Includes contractual plans, dual-purpose funds, tax-exempt bond funds, exchange funds, and Canadian funds. Available from IDD Inc., 150 Broadway, New York, N.Y. 10038.

Stock Sales on the New York Stock Exchange

This service will log volume, price, and time of individual transactions each day. Available from Francis Emory Fitch, 80 Broad Street, New York, N.Y. 10004.

The Investment Companies International Yearbook

A reference to the international investment company industry that contains prospectus-type data, including performance, on over 1,800 open- and closed-end mutual funds and investment companies in the United States, Canada, and thirty-four other countries. Available from Scheiman Ciaranella International Ltd., 505 Park Avenue, New York, N.Y. 10022.

Index

229